CAREER RESILIENCE

STRATEGIES TO GROW IN A CONSTANTLY EVOLVING MARKET

**VINAY
SAINI**

ISBN
Hardcase 979-8-89673-722-3
Paperback 979-8-89610-974-7

Disclaimer

This book is founded on my extensive personal knowledge and professional experiences, as well as the valuable insights I've gained from discussions with industry leaders and mentoring numerous individuals throughout my career. The strategies, concepts, and ideas presented here reflect my in-depth journey and expertise, honed over years of successfully navigating the complexities of a rapidly evolving industry.

Please note that the information presented in this book is not associated with any of my current or previous employers. The views expressed are entirely my own and do not represent the positions or opinions of any organization I have been affiliated with. This book is intended as a resource for individuals seeking to thrive in their careers, and any reference to businesses, strategies, or market conditions is purely anecdotal and not tied to any specific corporate entity.

Author – Vinay Saini

Dedication

This book is lovingly dedicated to the unwavering blessings of my parents, Mrs. Kaushalya Saini and Mr. Siri Ram Saini, whose guidance and values have beautifully shaped my journey. I also dedicate it to my beloved wife, Sowbhagya, whose endless love and encouragement light up my daily adventures. Finally, I dedicate it to my wonderful children, Vihaan and Pranav, whose boundless curiosity and enthusiasm inspire me to keep pushing forward. This work wouldn't exist without you — thank you for being my strength and inspiration!

Contents

About the Author 7

Preface 9

Designed for Quick Learning: Simple, Short Chapters...............11

Giving Back with a Purpose.. 13

How to Get Maximum Benefit from This Book 15

Section 1: Mastering the Business Landscape

Chapter 1   Business Fundamentals – Profit,
              Purpose, and Value...................................... 18

Chapter 2   Business Acumen – Understanding the
              Big Picture 28

Chapter 3   Shifting Perspectives – From Job
              Security to Skill Security.............................36

Chapter 4   Value Creation – Beyond Just Doing
              Your Job 44

Chapter 5   Networking for Success – Creating a
              Support System 51

Chapter 6   Personal Branding – Presenting Yourself
              for Success 59

Section 2: Cultivating Personal Excellence

Chapter 7   Emotional Intelligence (EI) –
Navigating People and Situations...................68

Chapter 8   Collaborate, Not Compete – Thriving
Together 77

Chapter 9   Mentoring – Building Success by
Lifting Others...86

Chapter 10   Lifelong Learning – Your Key to Staying
Relevant..95

Chapter 11   Mindfulness at Work – Finding Calm
Amidst Chaos 104

Chapter 12   Navigating the Unknown – Dealing with
Ambiguity 112

Embracing Change: Your Path to Growth and Resilience.......... 121

About the Author

Vinay Saini is a globally recognized expert with over two decades of experience navigating and shaping the ever-evolving professional and technological landscape. A visionary strategist and problem-solver, Vinay has partnered with organizations across industries to address their most pressing challenges, consistently delivering transformative results.

With a remarkable portfolio of over 100 filed patents, Vinay is a trailblazer in innovation. He is known for pushing the boundaries of possibility. His deep commitment to mentoring has helped countless professionals elevate their careers, equipping them with the skills and insights needed to thrive in uncertain times.

As a sought-after international speaker, Vinay shares his expertise on technology, leadership, and resilience, inspiring audiences to embrace change and unlock their potential. Renowned for his ability to foster growth and collaboration, Vinay brings a unique blend of experience, creativity, and forward-thinking to every endeavor.

In this book, Vinay thoughtfully shares his insights and experiences to support professionals in adapting to and thriving in challenging times

Preface

In today's fast-paced world, technology is advancing like never before. Thanks to automation, artificial intelligence, and other innovations, jobs that once seemed secure are transforming or disappearing altogether. This evolution can lead to uncertainty and disrupt the conventional routes to success we've been taught to pursue.

But change doesn't have to be something we fear. It opens opportunities for those willing to adapt, learn, and cultivate the right mindset. This book is not about chasing the latest technology trends; it's about understanding how to stay relevant and successful in any era, no matter how much the world shifts around us.

You'll find guidance on developing vital behavioral traits that help you thrive—resilience, adaptability, and a growth mindset, to name a few. These qualities are crucial in navigating a career landscape shaped by continuous disruption. I've also included practical strategies for fostering growth, adaptability, and resilience while emphasizing the importance of understanding business dynamics and aligning your efforts with broader organizational goals. These strategies will help you navigate challenges even when they initially seem overwhelming.

This book is a roadmap for a fulfilling career in a rapidly changing world. It's about more than just surviving change—it's about using it to propel yourself forward, to grow in ways you never thought possible.

I invite you to explore these insights with an open mind. I hope that by the end, you'll feel equipped and inspired to face change and master it.

Let's embark on this journey together.

Designed for Quick Learning: Simple, Short Chapters

I've lovingly designed this book with short, clear chapters because I know that, like me, you're busy. When you're seeking growth, especially during challenging times, you need advice that's quick to digest and ready to apply. Each chapter is crafted to provide you with straightforward insights and actionable steps, without any unnecessary fluff.

You'll find that you can read a chapter in just a few minutes, absorb the key ideas, and put them to work right away in your life and career. This isn't a book you'll have to slog through; it's one you can dip into, revisit, and draw inspiration from whenever you need a little boost or a fresh perspective. In uncertain times, it's often the simple, direct advice that makes the biggest difference. That's why I've kept each chapter concise and purposeful, offering you only the essentials to help you keep growing, no matter what challenges come your way.

Giving Back with a Purpose

Every penny earned from this book will be devoted to uplifting underprivileged children and supporting orphanages, ensuring they receive the daily care and education they deserve. I genuinely believe that everyone should have access to knowledge and opportunities. Through this effort, I aspire to make a significant impact on the lives of young individuals who deserve a radiant future. Growing up, my family has always inspired me to give back and contribute positively to our society, and this initiative is my way of honoring those cherished values. I'm grateful for your support on this wonderful journey to create a positive change. Together, let's open doors for those who need it the most!

How to Get Maximum Benefit from This Book

Swami Vivekananda, a remarkable Indian philosopher and author, once shared an incredible insight: while you can read, listen, and observe many things, the benefits come when you experience and put your learnings into action. This book explores several concepts, and practicing what you learn here is essential as a reader. This book is designed to be accessible to a wide range of readers, whether you're just starting your career or looking to navigate a changing job market. While some foundational topics are covered early on, they are essential for setting the stage for the following deeper strategies. By reading the book in its entirety, you'll gain a comprehensive understanding of how to adapt, grow, and thrive in challenging times. Each section builds on the last, ensuring that you have the tools to succeed in both the broader business context and your personal career development. I'd suggest reading through the entire book first, then highlighting the chapters that resonate with your goals and areas for improvement. Revisit those chapters and focus on integrating the lessons into your daily life. Creating a list of action items can be a great way to set achievable outcomes. Try to stick with these practices for at least a month so they become a part of your routine. To make this easier, I've included a simple exercise blueprint at the end of each chapter to help you get started.

This book is divided into two distinct yet complementary sections to equip you with the tools you need for success. The first section, **"Mastering the Business Landscape,"** focuses on understanding the broader business landscape, including how company strategies are changing in response to technology, aligning your personal goals with these strategies, and creating value through personal branding and networking. These chapters will help you navigate the corporate world, ensuring you are in tune with industry needs and ready to contribute in a way that resonates with current market demands.

The second section, **"Cultivating Personal Excellence,"** focuses on the personal traits and mindsets that will set you apart, even in the most uncertain times. Here, you'll explore emotional intelligence, collaboration, mentoring, mindfulness, and the importance of continuous learning. These chapters will help you develop the inner strength to handle challenges, adapt to change, and seize opportunities.

By breaking the book into these two categories, you gain a holistic approach to career resilience. The first set of chapters will empower you to understand the big picture, while the second set equips you with the skills and mindset to stay agile and adaptable. This combination creates a robust foundation for surviving and thriving in a world of uncertainty.

Wishing you a rewarding learning experience!

Section 1

MASTERING THE BUSINESS LANDSCAPE

In this set of chapters, you will discover the secrets behind the rapid shifts in technology and market forces reshaping industries. You will gain a deep understanding of how companies are evolving and how you can align your career with these changes. From decoding business strategies to creating value through personal branding and networking, these chapters will provide you with the tools to position yourself for success. You will learn how to tap into the changing business landscape, ensuring that you are not just keeping up with the curve, but staying ahead of it. The first few chapters focus on business strategy—don't skip them! Some think this isn't their area and miss out, which can limit growth. Understanding the bigger picture helps align your work with company goals and uncover new opportunities in any role.

Get ready to adopt a strategic mindset that will empower you to contribute meaningfully and gain a competitive edge in your field.

CHAPTER 1

Business Fundamentals – Profit, Purpose, and Value

In this chapter, we will discuss:

- Business and how it operates.
- Why business operations require employee adaptation.

Many of us might not think much about the complexities of business processes and operations in the early stages of our careers. It's common to get caught up in the excitement of landing that first job and dreaming about how to spend our paychecks! I was definitely in the same boat, and I genuinely have no regrets about that. We all deserve some time to enjoy life without too much worry about the finer details. However, as we become more involved and are encouraged to step outside our designated roles, it's easy to feel lost. I often found myself puzzled by how the different departments were structured and how each contributed to the company's overall success. I would hear my seniors discussing various leaders, their strategies, and how their teams worked together to drive the company's goals. This helped me better understand the business and its unique facets.

Welcome to this first chapter! This chapter lays the essential foundation for understanding the core components of any business that drive organizational success. Without grasping how businesses operate at their core, it becomes challenging to adapt to shifting market dynamics and evolving companies. As you progress through the book, the strategies and personal traits covered will build upon this understanding, enabling you to navigate through changes like technological disruptions, market shifts, and layoffs. Recognizing the importance of value creation and aligning yourself with your organization's goals will be crucial for surviving and thriving in times of uncertainty and transformation.

What is a Business?

In its simplest form, ***'Business is a process that can be repeated to generate income.'*** This definition is simple yet incredibly powerful. If your process isn't repeatable or doesn't generate profit, it's not truly a business. You might be engaging in it as a hobby or charity instead. Most of us are working professionals connected with some form of business. Consider your organization: it likely has products or services and processes to create and deliver them and charge customers accordingly. We all play a part in various stages of such a business. As you'll learn in the next chapter, aspects like products, services, methods of service, and pricing can shift with changing market conditions, consumer buying patterns, and technological advancements. Whenever there are changes in people, processes, or technology, it's essential to realign things to ensure that processes remain repeatable and profitable. Although this might not be a typical business book, this chapter aims to introduce you to concepts that are readily observable in the world around you.

Let's explore the essential business principles together in a way that's easy to understand. While some of you may already be familiar with these concepts from your industry experience, this overview provides a valuable refresher. In the subsequent chapters, we will discuss the personal traits necessary for success in an ever-evolving environment. A solid grasp of these business fundamentals will empower you to navigate the complexities of today's dynamic landscape effectively. Understanding basic principles equips us to engage meaningfully in our roles—employees or leaders—and remain attuned to the shifting business climate and its influence on our responsibilities. Additionally, embracing the necessity of adaptation is essential in this ever-changing context.

Through this exploration, I aim to instill confidence in your ability to thrive amidst these changes and guide you toward more incredible professional growth and resilience.

Let's delve together, starting with key business characteristics.

Value Creation

Every business is about creating a product or service that addresses a challenge or brings value to people's lives. Value creation is at the core of any business; it's the process of creating something that customers find helpful, desirable, or valuable enough to pay for. This value could be a product, a service, or a solution to a problem, and it's what ultimately drives a business's success. However, as customer preferences shift, technology advances, and competition grows, companies often need to adapt how they create value to stay relevant. For example, if customers start preferring eco-friendly products or digital services, a business may need to rethink its offerings to meet these demands. Typically, a business engages in market research to gain insights into what people or industries need, tailoring their products accordingly. This must be an ongoing effort as needs change over time. The businesses that struggle to create value for their customers often face tough times in the market. Staying adaptable and ready to adjust your offerings based on shifts in consumer behavior is essential. This adaptation requires employees to learn new skills, embrace new technologies, and sometimes even change their organizational roles. As a result, value creation is crucial for a company's growth and pushes employees to evolve, helping the business and its people stay resilient and competitive in a changing market. Take a moment to think about the organization you are part of and the specific needs it fulfills through its products and services.

Value creation is enabled by various other traits, such as:

Adaptability and Agility: To generate value effectively, organizations must be flexible and responsive to fluctuations in market demands and technological advancements. Adaptability enables organizations to adjust their offerings or introduce innovative products and services, ensuring they consistently fulfill customer expectations.

Customer-centricity: Recognizing and prioritizing customer needs is critical to creating value. By addressing customer challenges and preferences, businesses can customize their products and services to enhance relevance and satisfaction, ultimately generating more substantial value.

Innovation and Growth: Innovation serves as a fundamental catalyst for generating new value. By investing in novel concepts and creative problem-solving approaches, organizations can broaden their product offerings and effectively address unmet needs, thereby maintaining a dynamic and competitive value proposition.

Value Delivery

Delivering value is all about ensuring that a business's amazing benefits reach its customers seamlessly and dependably. This includes everything from crafting products to managing logistics, offering friendly customer support, and upholding exceptional quality and service standards. Customers appreciate reliability and convenience when accessing what they've invested in.

Delivering value also means finding just the right price for your product or service—pricing plays a vital role in how customers see that value. Even if a product perfectly meets customer needs and is consistently delivered, if the price doesn't match what customers expect or are willing to spend, they might not view it as valuable. It's essential that pricing reflects the quality, convenience, and benefits of your offering, striking a balance between being affordable and meeting business goals. As customer expectations evolve, market competition grows, and new technologies come into play, companies often adjust their pricing to stay in the game. For instance, with the rise of digital services and online shopping, customers may anticipate lower prices or more flexible payment options. This pushes companies to rethink their pricing strategies and tweak their delivery and support processes to keep up with these trends.

In simple terms, your product must deliver the same value to customers at a lower price compared to your competition or offer greater value, even if it's a bit more expensive. This scenario can be seen as an opportunity for beneficial transformations within your organization, as shifts in product offerings and market segments may occur if customers discover similar value at a lower price or more excellent value at a marginally higher cost. This mindset applies to us as shoppers as well. When we buy household items, we often adopt a similar approach to comparing different products. We assess the value we receive from an item against its cost. Every organization seeks its employees' contributions to enhance value and reduce production costs. Consistently delivering the expected value efficiently is crucial for a company's reputation. In response, employees must evolve by acquiring new skills, adopting digital tools, or discovering cost-effective delivery methods. Thus, effectively providing value necessitates constant attention to pricing, ensuring customers perceive worth in the product, ultimately fostering business growth and employee adaptability.

Additional traits that enhance value delivery include:

Operational Efficiency: Efficient operations are crucial for promptly and cost-effectively delivering value. Streamlining processes, reducing waste, and optimizing resources help ensure that value is delivered consistently and at scale, enhancing customer satisfaction and reliability.

Resilience and Change Management: A company's ability to stay stable amidst disruptions is crucial for effective delivery. Strong resilience and change management enable organizations to uphold service levels during turbulent times, ensuring uninterrupted value delivery.

Strategic Thinking and Big Picture Awareness: Consistently delivering value necessitates a clear grasp of long-term objectives and cross-departmental alignment. Strategic thinking enables companies to allocate resources effectively, foresee challenges, and focus on providing persistent value to customers.

Profits and Financial Stability

Profits and financial stability are fundamental goals for any business, representing its ability to earn more than it spends and maintain resources to operate and grow over time. Profits allow companies to invest in new products, improve services, expand operations, and reward employees. Financial stability ensures that a business can weather economic shifts, competitive pressures, or unforeseen challenges.

However, achieving profitability and stability isn't just about generating revenue; it requires managing costs, making intelligent investments, and adapting to market changes. As customer preferences evolve and technology advances, companies may need to rethink allocating resources or setting pricing to remain profitable without compromising value delivery. Employees play a critical role in this process by finding ways to work efficiently, embracing cost-saving technologies, and supporting initiatives contributing to sustainable growth. Profits and stability, therefore, are measures of a company's success and motivators for employees to grow alongside the business, ensuring long-term resilience in a dynamic market.

You may notice that organizations strive to improve their profit margins year after year. However, fluctuating markets can affect the profits of every organization. This connects back to the critical concepts of value creation and value delivery. Some organizations might choose to shut down or sell off parts of the business that aren't performing well, and these decisions can also impact the employees and leaders. While most of us aren't finance experts, having a basic understanding of key terms like EBITDA, Operating Profit Margin, and Cash Flow, as well as how to interpret financial statements, can be very beneficial. Employees need to be conscious of cost efficiency and resource optimization. A cost-effective approach doesn't mean cutting corners but making smart choices, which requires financial awareness and a strategic mindset.

Additional traits that help with profits and financial stability include:

Ethics and Responsibility: Sustainable profitability thrives when businesses embrace ethical practices and social responsibility. When companies choose to operate ethically, they create a solid foundation of trust with their customers, fostering brand loyalty that often results in more stable and lasting profits.

Innovation and Growth: Reinvesting profits opens the door to innovation, setting off an incredible cycle in which financial sustainability paves the way for growth and new value creation. This ongoing commitment to reinvestment not only nurtures profitability but also boosts our competitive edge and helps us expand into new markets.

Customer-Centricity: Focusing on the customer experience really boosts loyalty, which in turn helps grow our revenue. When we adopt a customer-centric approach, we not only keep our customers coming back but also reduce turnover and increase their lifetime value. All these factors work together to ensure sustainable profits.

At the heart of every successful business lies the trio of Value Creation, Value Delivery, and Profits. To reach and uphold these goals, embracing traits like adaptability, customer focus, innovation, operational efficiency, resilience, ethical practices, and strategic alignment is essential. No matter their position, every employee plays a vital role in embodying these principles. For instance, team members can foster adaptability by being eager to learn new skills, support customer focus by being attentive to client needs, or boost operational efficiency by discovering ways to simplify tasks.

The three pillars can be summarized as follows:

> **"Create and deliver value at a price that customers appreciate, thereby generating profits for the organization."**

Understanding the core principles that underpin a company's decisions is crucial for anyone seeking to navigate the complex landscape of modern business. Gripping the foundational reasons behind these choices illuminates the company's strategic direction and the various pathways that lie ahead. In summary, cultivating an understanding of these core principles does more than clarify the company's intentions; it empowers you to become an active participant in shaping the future for yourself and your organization. This knowledge may unlock potential in your career and the business landscape at large.

<u>**Exercise**</u>

Task 1: Determine your organization's primary and supporting businesses.

Task 2: Determine how value creation and delivery functions within your sub-organization.

Task 3: Identify the main business function that most of your work aligns with.

Task 4: Review the financial metrics for the organization from recent quarters.

CHAPTER 2

Business Acumen – Understanding the Big Picture

In this chapter, we will explore:

- The importance of grasping business models, market trends, and organizational strategies.
- How can individuals align their work with their organization's broader vision and strategy?

These are transformative times. Markets fluctuate, and new technologies arise every few months. Once considered futuristic, terms like AI and GenAI quickly become part of our reality. Organizations need to adjust to these changes, and you may have observed a continuous flow of adjustments and realignments across all sectors. This leads to constant updates in a company's strategies and ever-changing targets. In such situations, it is critical to monitor how your company responds to these changes and to consistently evolve its approach strategy.

A company may adjust its product or service strategy by introducing new offerings, combining existing services, or discontinuing elements that no longer align with future goals. It is essential to recognize that every organization aims to generate profits and expects its employees to play a role in that pursuit. Business acumen is not just for the executives but for everyone in the organization. Regardless of your role, it's vital to understand market trends, the business model your organization is adopting, and the specific strategy your group or organization implements. Let us look at some of the key concepts and how these impact us.

Business Acumen

It is about understanding how a company works and makes money. It's knowing what the company does, how it sells its products or services, and what it needs to be successful. This will help you make intelligent decisions at work that align with the company's goals. A common question I get, especially from individual contributors, is how we can start building our business acumen and where to begin. Here are a few actions you can take:

- Get to know your company's strategies, mission, and vision statements—they're usually shared on different media platforms. In this digital age, finding this information is a breeze with an online search. Just take some time to carefully explore both your company's internal and external web pages.
- It is beneficial to seek an outside-in perspective to gain a comprehensive understanding of your organisation's position in the market. Reading insights from business analysts can reveal how they perceive your company among competitors and within the broader industry landscape.
- Once you've clearly understood your company's direction, it's essential to see how your specific function or team fits within that strategy. A great way to do this is by tuning in to your leaders during update calls or meetings. You'll notice they often share important keywords, like specific technologies and areas of focus. Hearing these terms frequently among aligned leaders is a wonderful indication of the company's path forward. Plus, remember that you always have

the opportunity to ask questions during meetings or in one-on-one sessions with your leader. They're there to help you navigate this journey together.

After gaining a deep understanding of your organization and team's strategic approach, it is recommended to reassess the current initiatives and projects. This reassessment helps determine if they truly align with your company's growth strategy. For instance, one of my mentees is a talented developer who possesses extensive knowledge of the latest technology; he invests considerable time creating impressive projects using these new concepts. Unfortunately, his management, although impressed with his work, struggles to support or advance his ideas because they do not align with the organization's goals. Consequently, despite his efforts in learning and developing new ideas, he feels stagnant in his growth within the organization. This situation clearly illustrates the importance of aligning personal aspirations with the organization's strategy, a scenario that many of us can relate to. In such instances, it is crucial to align with our organizational needs or consider exploring other opportunities that may be a better fit. If you choose to join a different team or organization, it's vital to align with their business priorities. This way, you'll contribute effectively and build strong connections.

Business Model

It is essentially a plan that outlines how a company operates and generates revenue. It defines the products or services the company offers, who its customers are, how it delivers value to those customers, and how it earns money. In simple terms, a business model explains:

- What the company sells (product or service or both).
- Who it sells to (target customers or market).

- How it sells (distribution channels or sales methods like subscriptions).
- How it makes money (pricing strategy, revenue streams, etc.).

For example, in the IT industry, companies like Microsoft offer software like Office 365 through a subscription model. Instead of buying the software outright, customers pay a monthly or annual fee. This business model generates consistent revenue over time.

You might notice that the business model changes occasionally, keeping pace with the company's evolving strategy. Once you grasp this model, it can unfold exciting opportunities for you to innovate and enhance it even more. For instance, if you're part of an e-commerce platform, understanding that customers appreciate speedy delivery (just like in Amazon's business model) can help you focus on boosting the logistics chain instead of wandering into unrelated areas. This focused innovation drives growth and helps your company thrive in the right direction. This also signifies that your contributions are positively impacting the company, leading to recognition of your work and effort.

Market Trends

It is the general direction in which a particular market, industry, or technology moves over time. Changes in consumer behavior, technological advances, economic factors, and industry shifts shape trends. These trends influence what products and services are in demand, how businesses operate, and how they position themselves in the market. Market trends can be categorized into several types:

- **Technology Trends**: Advancements like artificial intelligence (AI), 5G, or cloud computing.

- **Consumer Behaviour Trends**: Shifts in how consumers make purchasing decisions, like a preference for online shopping or sustainable products.
- **Economic Trends**: Economic changes affecting purchasing power, inflation, and industry growth.
- **Regulatory Trends**: Changes in government regulations or industry standards that affect how businesses must operate.

Understanding market trends in your area is essential. If you're not in tune with these trends, you might find that your skills or approach drift away from what the market and your company need to thrive. In challenging times, being innovative can set companies apart—it's often what helps you succeed when facing difficult situations. When employees bring forth ideas that align with market trends, they provide valuable solutions that help the business navigate difficulties. You will notice that such employees thrive even in more challenging times.

Sometimes, we unintentionally create obstacles in our minds when aligning with the organization's strategy, often due to misinformation. While conducting market research and chatting with colleagues in the same industry, it can be easy to make assumptions and conclude that your organization might be making the wrong decisions. In a large organization, many factors and insights may not be visible to employees or even senior management. Some of this information might be confidential and could prompt necessary strategy realignments. It might come from a market research report or even pending acquisition or divestment plans. Feel free to ask questions and explore the right channels for clarification. Embracing change can be challenging, but keeping an open mind and not holding back is essential. Assumptions can make it tricky to fully grasp the company's goals, which might lead to misunderstandings about your leadership's direction. This can create confusion and make it harder for individuals and teams to stay aligned.

Aligning with Organizational Objectives

Here are several actions you can take to remain aligned with the organization's objectives:

Goal Alignment: Consider how your personal goals can align with the company's vision. If your company emphasizes innovation or customer satisfaction, your projects and daily tasks should resonate with those values. For instance, if the organization is all about digital transformation, take a moment to explore how you can play a vital role in that exciting journey.

SMART Goals: Embrace the **SMART** (Specific, Measurable, Achievable, Relevant, and Time-bound) goal framework to help align your objectives with broader company goals. Use metrics to measure the impact and ensure your efforts drive meaningful results.

Performance Check-ins: It's essential to have regular conversations with your manager to ensure your efforts align with the department and company goals. Feel free to ask for feedback on fine-tuning your contributions to support the organization's strategy better.

Cross-Departmental Awareness: It is essential to recognize the impact of your work on other departments and acknowledge how their contributions align with the organization's overarching strategy. Successful collaboration guarantees that various organizational segments collectively strive toward shared objectives.

Adopt a flexible strategy: Businesses frequently modify their approaches in response to market dynamics or operational requirements. Remain open-minded and prepared to realign your focus with emerging priorities.

Assess and readjust: Regularly evaluate your efforts to confirm their alignment with the overarching organizational strategy, particularly following any strategic modifications.

In conclusion, grasping business acumen and organizational strategy is essential for personal growth during favorable and challenging times. It empowers individuals to make informed decisions, align their efforts with company objectives, and enhance business success. During prosperous times, this knowledge fosters performance and career advancement, while in challenging periods, it aids in navigating uncertainty, prioritizing essential initiatives, and adjusting to evolving conditions. This adaptability enhances individuals' resilience, increases their value, and equips them to drive success regardless of external factors.

<u>Exercise</u>

Task 1: Jot down your company's mission and its future goals for the upcoming years.

Task 2: List the critical priority areas for your organization.

Task 3: Translate how your role can contribute to the targets identified by your company.

Task 4: Evaluate how your existing work and initiatives align with your organization's strategy

CHAPTER 3

Shifting Perspectives – From Job Security to Skill Security

In this chapter, we will explore:

- Transferable and evolving skills in the current era of rapid changes.
- Change in the hiring perspective of employers.

Job stability is a significant concern for numerous professionals. We often seek positions in stable companies, hoping for organic growth, long-term employment, and benefits that help ensure financial safety and a balanced lifestyle. However, the fast-moving world of technology, automation, and globalization has shaken up the traditional job model. Rather than focusing on job security, attention is shifting toward an even more engaging concept: skill security.

Skill security is all about staying employable and adaptable in our fast-paced job market. Continuously developing and upgrading your transferable skills is a wonderful way to prepare for whatever comes your way. Unlike traditional job security, which often keeps you in a single position or company with a specific type of work, skill security benefits from a rich and diverse skill set that applies across various industries, roles, and technologies. It fosters a mindset of lifelong learning and adaptability, empowering you to navigate career transitions, embrace exciting technological changes, and confidently respond to shifts in the economy.

Impact of Strategy Changes on Jobs

In the previous chapter, we established that the landscape of organizational strategies and alignments is not static; it is, in fact, a dynamic entity that continuously evolves in response to market demands, technological advancements, and shifting consumer behavior. This ongoing evolution necessitates a fundamental shift in direction regarding the focus and objectives of companies. Organizations can no longer afford to be complacent or adhere rigidly to outdated practices. Instead, they must adapt swiftly to remain relevant and competitive.

The first critical action an organization must undertake in this transformative journey is to align its workforce with the newly identified products and services that resonate with the current market landscape. This alignment is not merely about adjusting job descriptions; it is an imperative that requires organizations to initiate production or commence service delivery in these new areas as expeditiously and efficiently as possible. The urgency of this task cannot be overstated, as market windows of opportunity can be fleeting.

To meet this demand, organizations often find that they must engage in rapid training of existing employees, equipping them with new skills that are necessary to navigate these changing waters. Alternatively, they may decide to look outward, recruiting individuals who possess the specific expertise needed to drive these new initiatives. This dual approach ensures that organizations maintain a competitive edge, but it also introduces a level of uncertainty in employment conditions.

In their quest for agility, organizations may be less inclined to offer guarantees of permanent positions during such transitions. Instead, they may favor the use of contractual jobs, which allow for greater flexibility in workforce management. This shift underscores a broader trend; organizations are increasingly prioritizing employees who demonstrate a high degree of adaptability and commitment to ongoing skill enhancement. These attributes are seen as essential for movement across different teams and roles within the organization.

Organizational restructuring often accompanies these changes. As companies pivot toward their new focus, they may reassign employees to roles that align more closely with the updated objectives. This reallocation is not arbitrary; it is a strategic move to harness the strengths of agile employees who can thrive in the face of change. Unfortunately, this reality means that during such phases of restructuring, those employees who fail to demonstrate agility and adaptability may face dismissal.

Thus, we confront a sobering truth of our times. The landscape of employment within organizations is changing rapidly, and the survival of both the company and its workforce may hinge upon the ability to pivot, learn, and adapt. In this relentless march of progress, what was once a dependable job may now be a precarious undertaking, shaped by the ever-evolving demands of the modern business environment.

Adapting to the Skills Security Concept

Different generations have traditionally viewed job security differently. For example, Gen Z (born after 1997) tends to favor skill security and flexibility, while older generations may have preferred long-term employment. For Millennials (born between 1981 and 1996) and the older generation, loyalty to a single employer was expected, and companies often rewarded this loyalty with pensions, benefits, and a clear career ladder. For many in these generations, job security meant staying in one role or company for years, even decades. This perspective was shaped by a time when industries were relatively stable, and job roles did not change as rapidly as today. Currently, economic recessions, technological disruptions, and the gig economy have shown us that long-term job security is often uncertain. Even within the same organization, you should look at taking on new responsibilities and learning new things. A focus on skill security can bridge this gap by encouraging all generations to see the value of continuous learning and adaptability. Let us look at some steps you can take to strengthen skill security in an unstable job market.

Explore Emerging Trends: Staying up-to-date on your industry's direction is essential. You can make informed decisions about your career path by identifying the skills that are in demand. A simple way to do this is by quickly looking at internal and external job portals and filtering positions that align with your experience and field. This can give you valuable insights into what recruiters are currently seeking. Plus, it's a great idea to maintain a current copy of your resume and compare it with the job market. This way, you can easily spot any gaps in your skill set and work toward filling them.

Invest in Transferable Soft Skills: Communication and collaboration skills are valued in nearly every industry, helping you adapt to various roles. Companies truly appreciate employees who can work across teams, communicate effectively, and handle client interactions. From my experience, candidates with strong communication skills often excel—not necessarily because they are more intelligent but because they can express their ideas clearly. A great way to enhance these skills is by enrolling in training programs and, most importantly, practicing regularly.

Investment of time and money in such transferable skills always benefits.

Engage in Continuous Learning: It's possible that you've reached the limits of your current position because some of your skills and knowledge may be a bit outdated. If you're looking to explore new opportunities, the best approach is to learn new skills that can open up those pathways for you. Embrace online courses, join workshops, and participate in training programs that match current industry demands. Online platforms such as Coursera, Udacity, and LinkedIn Learning provide courses across various relevant subjects. With numerous resources available, it is easy to gain new skills today. All you need is a plan and dedicated time for learning integrated into your daily routine.

Understanding the Employer's Perspective

It is crucial to understand the changing perspectives of employers. In recent years, many have shifted their focus from traditional qualifications, such as years of experience or specific job titles, to candidates' skill sets, adaptability, and potential. With the rapid advancements in technology, automation, and artificial intelligence, nearly every industry is undergoing significant transformation. Skills previously deemed essential may quickly diminish in importance while new talents remain in constant demand. Companies seek candidates who can learn swiftly and adapt to new technologies and methodologies. Rather than merely hiring individuals with extensive experience in a particular domain, recruiters prioritize those who demonstrate the ability to adapt to and master new tools and techniques.

Numerous organizations are willing to employ candidates who may lack substantial experience but exhibit considerable potential and possess fundamental skills. They have increasingly come to appreciate critical competencies, often providing training to bridge skill gaps. The relationship between a company and a candidate is mutually beneficial, as the organization secures an individual who possesses a comprehensive understanding of emerging technologies. In contrast, the candidate can apply their knowledge in practice and enhance their learning. Therefore, individuals must commence their education on new technologies and trends pertinent to their organization at the earliest possible opportunity.

Many people take pride in their experience in one specific area, sometimes believing it makes them irreplaceable and stopping them from learning new things. However, it is noteworthy that numerous occupations available today did not exist merely a few years prior. In this fast-paced world, organizations seek individuals who can adapt and grow into future roles instead of just meeting the current job requirements. After all, having experience in one position doesn't always guarantee success in a constantly changing environment. Experience, when combined with continuous learning, creates a path to success. New waves of technology come every year, and companies don't want to miss the opportunities to ride them. This results in sudden requirements for specific skill sets, and as the technology is new, they often don't find many experienced people available to hire externally or internally. In such cases, individuals ready to take up the challenge and try new things usually find a place in the right team. Many such waves may not last long, but you must be prepared to contribute in the best possible ways.

In summary, adaptability represents our most significant asset as we navigate rapid changes. Professionals who cultivate skill security and actively pursue knowledge across diverse fields will survive in today's job market and truly thrive. It is also essential to strike a balance; your career aspirations should align with your personal well-being. As the workforce continues to evolve, individuals who nurture both dimensions will be positioned to enjoy rewarding and enduring careers. One must refrain from establishing a mental blockade that prohibits the acquisition of new skills or the learning of new technologies. Anyone can develop new competencies with a systematic approach and a well-defined plan. Continually updating oneself and striving to become an improved version of oneself is imperative.

<u>**Exercise**</u>

Task 1: Identify the essential skills your industry requires currently and where you stand.

Task 2: List new skills you have acquired in the last year.

Task 3: Identify the roadblocks you typically face when acquiring a new skill, such as time constraints or lack of motivation.

Task 4: Note opportunities you could tap into or those you lost due to skill requirement changes in the last year.

Chapter 4

Value Creation – Beyond Just Doing Your Job

In this chapter, we will discuss:

- The importance of value creation in your day-to-day job.
- Approaching tasks with a mindset focused on value creation.

The first two chapters explored the significance of understanding the company strategy and its immediate priorities. We also emphasized the need for alignment regarding skill security amidst ongoing changes in the third chapter. Despite being part of the right team aligned with company goals, we sometimes struggle to grow. Employers seek individuals who transcend their job descriptions and add significant value to their work, colleagues, and leadership. You will notice that most companies have 360-degree feedback criteria for all employees. Positive feedback should come from everyone, including colleagues, subordinates, and supervisors. While there's no one-size-fits-all definition of 360-degree feedback, some organizations gather insights from various groups to assess your impact, even if those groups are not directly within your team. Others look at feedback beyond the organization, sometimes from partners or direct customers, to obtain a well-rounded view.

A mentor once said, "Vinay, always aim to contribute one level above your current position." He explained that performing at a higher level makes it easier for your leader and upper management to see you as a candidate for promotion. This straightforward yet impactful insight was one of the most valuable pieces of advice I've ever received. Many of us tend to confine ourselves to our current title's job description and responsibilities. I often hear some people say, "This isn't my job; this should be handled a level above me." I'm not suggesting we overburden ourselves by taking on someone else's work and stressing ourselves out. However, it's worth considering whenever we notice an opportunity that fits well into our work schedule.

When I shared the idea of demonstrating impact beyond our current roles with my mentee, she asked, "How can I find such opportunities?" It's amazing how much we can learn just by collaborating with someone with more experience. If you encounter someone working on a project that excites you, don't hesitate to offer your support. You could say, "I'm eager to assist with your idea! Just let me know how I can help." This small gesture can create new opportunities for you. Even if it doesn't lead to something immediately, there's a strong chance they will think of you when they need help next time, especially if your offer was sincere. The success of this approach also hinges on the personal brand you build within your organization, which we'll dive into in a later chapter. When those opportunities arise, be prepared to dedicate a few extra hours to lend your support. Those additional hours spent working alongside someone can truly make a difference. Once you start contributing in this way a couple of times, you might find that person begins to delegate more responsibilities to you. By taking this initiative, you've already created opportunities to shine beyond your current role. Just remember to ensure that your contributions are recognized and align with your organization's goals.

Approaches to Enhance the Value of Your Work

Here are some ways to enhance the value of your daily tasks.

Begin by Identifying Opportunities that Generate Value

Take a moment to jot down the areas where your unique skills can make a difference. Think about how you can boost efficiency, enhance productivity, or even spark some creative ideas. Companies appreciate insights that can drive revenue growth or reduce costs, resulting in savings. No matter your role—whether you're an individual contributor or a manager—you can contribute meaningfully to these efforts. You don't always have to propose new concepts; many ongoing initiatives align with these goals. It's essential to find opportunities to engage actively. Some of these initiatives may not directly relate to the organization's core business, like Corporate Social Responsibility (CSR), but they can still benefit the company and the community. Businesses that participate in CSR create positive impacts on society and the environment and enjoy significant business benefits, fostering a sustainable cycle of mutual advantage. It's crucial to align your efforts with the values your organization upholds.

Develop a Value-creating Mindset

We often get so caught up in the daily tasks that we forget to see how they contribute to creating value for our organization. It's so important that your role adds meaningful value. One helpful approach is to think about it in terms of dollar value. Consider how your daily work supports the organization in making or saving money or achieving key objectives. When taking on a new initiative or task, ask yourself, "How is this helping my organization?" If the answer isn't clear, don't hesitate to chat with your manager, mentor, or senior colleague. Adopting this mindset of adding value will guide you in choosing the right tasks and initiatives, ensuring you always make a tangible and meaningful contribution to your organization. I recently had a delightful coffee chat with a former colleague from my previous organization. He opened up about feeling lost in his current team and struggling to see how his work fits the company strategy. Even though he had seen updates about the company's changing direction in newspapers and online, he found it challenging to connect his day-to-day tasks to those big-picture changes. This caused him some confusion, making him feel like he wasn't aligning with the company's goals. I suggested that he have an open conversation with his management to clarify how his contributions tie into the company's strategy and explore ways he could add even more value. A few days later, when we chatted again, he felt so much more confident after discussing things with his management. He recognized the importance of his work to the company's broader mission. Not only did he feel valued, he also generated excellent ideas for amplifying his contributions and establishing himself as an essential asset, which I will explore further in the next section. Management and leaders in any organization must assist candidates at every level in understanding how their work connects to overall company objectives. If management isn't proactively engaged in this, don't hesitate to seek clarification. Ask how you can align your efforts and create value for the organization.

Establishing Yourself as a Valuable Asset

This step builds on that valuable mindset we've talked about and focuses on finding the right tasks to pursue. Once you've identified and engaged with these tasks, it's essential to show how your contributions positively affect your organization. Senior management really appreciates tangible outcomes, so it's helpful to have some data ready to support your ideas.

Simply being part of larger initiatives might not be enough; it's crucial to carve out your own position and take ownership of specific tasks within that broader set of activities. You'll make a meaningful impact by demonstrating your value as an asset to the team and the organization. I had the opportunity to be involved in a talent review for some candidates up for promotion. We were eager to gather insightful data about each candidate's contributions from their managers. One candidate stood out with a wealth of information—he seemed involved in nearly every initiative within the organization. At first, this was quite impressive! However, upon closer examination, we realized that while he enthusiastically promoted his involvement, his contributions to many of those initiatives were minimal, primarily as a participant. We decided to remove that candidate's name from the promotion list. We gently advised him to focus on making a meaningful impact, even just on a few items. It's all about having a targeted approach where your contributions are recognized as impactful. It is best to focus on fewer but more impactful tasks.

Regularly Evaluate the Value Generated

Keeping track of the unique value created through your work is essential. Record your projects, initiatives, and tasks every week. This simple practice benefits you in two ways: first, you'll have a complete list of your contributions, and second, you'll gain insights into the value generated by your actions. Sometimes, we get so engaged in one activity that we overlook other tasks that deserve our attention. For instance, one of our colleagues became excited about organizing fun events for the team and took the initiative to manage these activities repeatedly. After a few successful gatherings, he proudly earned the title of 'event organizer.' Even though he excelled in his other roles, the spotlight was mainly on those enjoyable events. He found himself drawn into tasks that didn't directly add value to the core business. During the performance review, this candidate could not map his efforts to the direct dollar value. This highlights the importance of prioritizing our time and focusing on tasks that genuinely contribute to our organization's success, especially during challenging times. Ultimately, your achievements will be compared with others and weighed against the dollar impact. Having a focused list and conducting regular assessments will help you avoid too much effort on trivial tasks.

In summary, we all know that time can feel like a precious resource. Creating value in your role is all about finding that sweet spot where you can balance tasks that uplift crucial areas of the organization, such as making our customers happy, boosting our efficiency, and sparking innovation. Consider setting up a simple assessment plan to keep improving and aligning your efforts. Regularly review your performance metrics, gather friendly feedback from peers and supervisors, and ensure you align with the organization's goals. This plan can help you focus on tasks that offer the most value, especially with our limited time. By sorting tasks based on their impact and urgency, you can dedicate your efforts to the activities that truly matter, ensuring your work addresses immediate needs and paves the way for our long-term success.

<u>Exercise</u>

Task 1: List activities and tasks from the last two months and their generated value.

Task 2: Assess the dollar value of your contributions in savings or revenue.

Task 3: Identify activities you lead that misalign with company goals.

Task 4: Identify opportunities for immediate contribution (items you've been procrastinating).

CHAPTER 5

Networking for Success – Creating a Support System

In this chapter, we will discuss:

- The significance of professional networking.
- Ways to expand your professional network.

One of my friends is a career coach at a well-known company. She provides coaching to diverse talent across various fields and helps people at all levels of their careers. We had a great conversation about how market needs are evolving and affecting different industries, such as IT and manufacturing. I asked her about the current job market in the IT industry, especially with all the excitement surrounding AI and Automation. She replied that it varies based on your skills, but more crucially, on your experience and salary expectations. However, what she told me next really resonated: "As we advance into more senior roles, most hires come from referrals and recommendations." It's essential to understand how critical it is to have a supportive network, both within your organization and with other companies in your field. You may have heard the saying, "Don't burn bridges when leaving your current role or organization." This emphasizes the value of maintaining those old connections while building new ones. The goal is to create bridges that endure and foster win-win situations for everyone involved. It's common to see talented individuals moving from one company to another within their fields.

A few years ago, I had the pleasure of working with a major mining customer on their transformation. We had wonderful conversations about their needs with their transformation officer and accomplished great work together. Not long after, the same individual transitioned to another mining organization with similar requirements and reached out to us right away for support with an even broader transformation opportunity. This was all thanks to the strong connection we had, not only through our professional interactions but also during friendly chats over coffee and lunch breaks. Of course, our connection ran deeper than those casual conversations; it was mainly due to the fantastic work my team and I did, helping them establish a vision that would make them one of the leading mines in the country. Throughout that project, I built great relationships with many of my sales, engineering, and services colleagues. Even nearly a decade later, we still connect for technical support, engage in discussions, and encourage each other's growth opportunities.

In my early career, networking wasn't my strong suit, and I'm still improving this skill today. I used to think that excelling in my job was sufficient. Although that belief held for the first few years, I soon recognized the crucial role of building a network. Success is not solely about performing well at work; it also involves exchanging ideas, discussing insights, and helping others grow. By engaging in these activities, a network will naturally form around you. The vital part is nurturing that network through positive contributions to others' lives. A few weeks ago, an old colleague who had left my company to launch his consulting firm called me for advice on a challenge he faced. I was happy to support him and share my thoughts. This connection stemmed from our prior agreement that he could reach out whenever he needed assistance. We had kept in touch through simple WhatsApp messages, exchanging New Year and festival greetings, which maintained our bond. A few days later, he called again, excited to share that he had resolved his issue and pleased his customer. Our discussion went beyond work; we also talked about family and friends, which was notable since we were never close friends or collaborated on projects at the same company.

Networking is a great way to discover industry trends, create new opportunities, and swiftly respond to changes. By building a solid network, you gain access to valuable experiences from others, acquire insights that could take years to gather, and keep yourself relevant in these unpredictable times. With new skills constantly emerging and the demand for adaptability growing, professionals must stay connected and informed. Networking with peers and seniors offers insights and access to their knowledge and connections.

Importance of Networking

Let's explore how networking contributes to career advancement in today's ever-changing environment.

Access to Opportunities: Most job and project opportunities are rarely advertised through traditional channels, leaving many seekers unaware of potential roles that suit their skills. Instead, these positions are often filled through referrals and personal recommendations, emphasizing the importance of networking in today's job market. When you cultivate a robust professional network, you significantly increase your chances of learning about job openings and specialized projects that may not be publicly listed. This network can consist of former colleagues, mentors, industry peers, and even acquaintances from educational experiences. By engaging in conversations, attending industry events, and connecting on platforms like LinkedIn, you can gain insights into roles and opportunities that align with your career aspirations. A strong network is an invaluable resource, allowing you to tap into the hidden job market where many exciting opportunities lie.

Knowledge Sharing: You can learn from others' successes and mistakes through networking, saving you valuable time and resources. This sharing goes both ways; when you offer your knowledge, you become a valuable resource to others. Networking opens up incredible opportunities for sharing ideas and experiences with people from various backgrounds and industries. By connecting with a broader community, you discover insights that you may not come across in your usual circles. For instance, hearing about creative practices others have put into action can spark inspiration, encouraging you to try out new strategies that can bring about even better solutions in your work. Moreover, sharing your knowledge not only helps others avoid potential pitfalls but also reinforces your expertise. Contributing your insights and experiences builds your reputation as a knowledgeable individual in your field. This reciprocal relationship fosters a supportive environment where individuals are encouraged to collaborate, seek advice, and share resources. Ultimately, knowledge sharing through networking cultivates a culture of continuous learning where everyone can grow and succeed together.

Professional Growth: Engaging with various perspectives and industries is crucial for personal and professional growth. When you expose yourself to different viewpoints, you challenge your assumptions and develop a more comprehensive understanding of the world around you. This diversity in thought can stimulate your creativity, enabling you to think outside the box and approach problems from unique angles. Regular interactions with individuals from various backgrounds create an environment where ideas can flourish. These exchanges can inspire you to explore new concepts, methods, or business practices, driving innovation in your projects. Additionally, collaboration with diverse teams fosters adaptability as you learn to navigate varied communication styles and work strategies.

Support System: Networking is vital during difficult times, serving as a crucial resource for emotional and practical assistance. When faced with challenges, such as job losses, having a network of individuals to connect with can significantly alleviate stress and open doors to new opportunities. These connections provide a sense of belonging and reassurance, reminding you that you are not alone in your struggles. Moreover, whether it involves brainstorming solutions to problems or sharing experiences, your network can offer diverse perspectives and advice that can help navigate through tough situations, including finding new career paths. Furthermore, engaging with others in your network can serve as a powerful source of encouragement, motivating you to persevere even when the going gets tough. The relationships you cultivate can be instrumental in your personal and professional growth, as they not only help you overcome obstacles, such as unemployment, but also contribute to a more fulfilling and enriched life overall.

Steps to Build Your Network

You'll notice that many executives enjoy meeting regularly for games or dinner. These gatherings allow them to share their experiences, explore new opportunities, and discuss market trends. Many conversations about hiring or job movements often start at these lively events. Building connections doesn't just happen; it requires effort and time.

In networking, people will admire you for your success and the skills and knowledge you bring to the table. Building genuine relationships allows people to appreciate the unique value you provide, fostering their admiration for your talents. They'll see you as someone they genuinely want to collaborate with and share with others, creating a lovely cycle that enhances your network. Plus, when people feel that you genuinely care about them as individuals rather than just as a means to an end, they are much more likely to collaborate.

Although it's simple to suggest, what actions can you take to build and expand your network? Let's look at some of them:

Be Present in Conversations: When you engage with someone, give them your full attention. Ask questions, show curiosity, and listen actively. This shows respect and fosters a deeper connection.

Follow Up with Thoughtfulness: After meeting someone, follow up with a note of appreciation or by sharing an article relevant to a topic you discussed. Thoughtful follow-ups show that you value the interaction.

Stay in Touch: Networking is not a one-time interaction but an ongoing process. Check in with people periodically, ask about their work, and be genuine in wanting to stay connected.

Be Honest About Your Skills and Limitations: Overstating your abilities or making false promises can damage trust. If you're transparent about your strengths and weaknesses, people will respect you more and feel confident recommending you to others.

Celebrate Others' Successes: When someone in your network achieves something, celebrate it with them. This helps you build goodwill and shows that you genuinely care about their success.

In conclusion, authentic networking anchored in mutual respect and reciprocity is a pathway to sustained success. Establishing such a network entails fostering a community of allies who assist one another in achieving growth and prosperity. Furthermore, it involves constructing a foundation of trust and reliability that will distinguish itself and persist in generating opportunities, even amidst the changing dynamics of the world.

<u>Exercise</u>

Task 1: Evaluate your professional connections within the organization.

Task 2: Create a list of professionals from other companies you can confidently contact for referrals.

Task 3: Reflect on your chances in the last six months to engage with former colleagues.

Task 4: Create a list of steps to re-establish your connections if you are not doing so already.

CHAPTER 6

Personal Branding – Presenting Yourself for Success

In this chapter, we will discuss:

- The significance of establishing a personal brand.
- Initiating the process of brand building.

Recently, I had an enlightening mentoring session with a mid-career employee from my organization who was struggling with stress about his role and growth path. He openly shared his experiences of burnout, stemming from an increasing workload. Despite his dedication, he expressed deep frustration, feeling unable to make the impact he desired. As part of a substantial team of around 40 individuals, he meticulously articulated the nature of his work and his skills. However, it became evident to me that amidst this talented group, he felt like just another cog in the wheel—one whose contributions were indistinguishable from those of his colleagues.

After listening attentively to him for a few minutes, I gently posed a couple of reflective questions designed to spark introspection: "Can you think of one or two things that your whole group relies on you for?" or "Where do people in your team, or even outside your group, come to you for suggestions or help?" His response came slowly as if he were untangling a complex web of thoughts. He took a brief pause, and then, with a furrowed brow, replied, "I don't think there's anything like that; I have all the same skills as the rest of my team."

At that moment, I perceived a deeper issue at play – he seemed to be missing a crucial element of his professional identity: a personal brand. This concept of personal branding is not just a trendy buzzword; it embodies the unique essence that distinguishes one individual from another in the bustling talent marketplace. Without a clear personal brand, it becomes all too easy to feel lost amidst a sea of similar capabilities and experiences.

I reflected on the importance of creating a distinct identity in the workplace—a positive persona that resonates with colleagues and stakeholders alike. A personal brand is a beacon, guiding others to recognize your value and contributions. It's about showcasing not only your skills and expertise but also the unique perspectives and passions you bring to your role. Without such a deliberate effort to carve out a positive identity, it's all too easy to blend into the crowd, which can exacerbate feelings of invisibility and disconnection in a large organization. Finding ways to highlight what makes you distinct is essential for both personal fulfillment and professional advancement.

In moments like these, mentorship can play a pivotal role, guiding individuals to recognize their strengths and leverage them in building a brand that is uniquely theirs. It's an ongoing journey that requires self-reflection and the courage to stand out. Understanding that we all possess unique qualities is critical to navigating our careers effectively and making the impact we desire—and that realization is worth pursuing. As you begin your journey toward personal branding, you might notice a fascinating transformation in your immediate environment. People around you are no longer passively existing; they are increasingly recognizing and becoming familiar with your brand. This is not a mere coincidence but a reflection of the consistency and dedication you've shown in your work and interactions.

Take a moment to look around your organization. Numerous individuals may stand out as experts in their respective fields. Some may have honed their skills in specific technologies, while others excel in the art of customer service, the nuances of sales, or the delicate dance of innovation. You'll often find individuals who excel at building strong connections with their colleagues, creating a beautiful tapestry of collaboration and friendship.

Regardless of your talents, there is a universal truth: when you consistently demonstrate positivity in your actions or achieve remarkable outcomes, you are, in essence, crafting a brand for yourself. This brand reflects your values, your skills, and the impact you leave on those around you. It is as if each positive interaction or successful project adds a brushstroke to the canvas of your professional identity.

Building a Brand Takes Time

It's important to recognize that building a brand isn't an overnight process — it doesn't happen at the flip of a switch. Instead, developing a brand that truly reflects your identity demands patience, dedication, and a steadfast commitment to consistency. As you consistently showcase excellence and maintain a positive attitude, you will gradually build a reputation that exudes authenticity and trust.

In essence, personal branding is a journey—a continuous process of self-discovery and engagement with the world around you. It invites you to invest time and energy, nurturing the relationships you build and the impressions you leave. So, embark on this endeavor with an open heart and a determined spirit, for the rewards of a well-established brand are truly invaluable.

In today's fast-paced and ever-evolving market, it is crucial to reflect on the brand you represent. Whether you already have an established brand or are in the formative stages of creating one, the journey to brand development is an ongoing process that requires thought and adaptation. If you already have a brand, consider yourself fortunate; you have a foundation upon which to build and expand. However, if you do not have a defined brand, now is the perfect opportunity to embark on this journey of self-identification and market positioning. Moreover, given the shifting tides of consumer preferences and industry dynamics, it becomes imperative to periodically reassess whether your brand remains relevant and appealing. For instance, if you once held the status of an expert in a technology that is now waning in relevance, it is essential to pivot and evolve your brand identity accordingly. The landscape of technology and consumer needs continuously changes, and so must your brand.

A simple yet effective way to breathe new life into your brand is to invest time in learning and mastering emerging skills. Identify adjacent technologies or the next iteration of the expertise you once possessed. By doing so, you position yourself not just as a follower in the industry, but as a forward-thinking leader who anticipates change and adapts to it.

In the upcoming chapter on continuous learning in this book, I will provide actionable tips and strategies for building upon your existing skills and embracing new opportunities for growth. Remember, regardless of the direction you choose to take, one undeniable truth remains: you must keep your brand vibrant and current.

In every business sector, logos, marketing strategies, and business approaches perpetually evolve to resonate with consumer demands. This same principle applies to our personal brands. Just as companies refresh their identities to stay relevant, we, too, must ensure that our brand reflects the current zeitgeist and effectively communicates our value.

Starting Your Brand Journey

Embrace the challenge. Your brand is not just a name or a logo; it is an ever-evolving narrative that tells the world who you are and what you stand for. Creating a strong, personal brand in an organization or industry is about building a reputation that reflects who you are, what you stand for, and the value you bring. Here are some simple steps to create and maintain a relevant personal brand.

- Consider your strengths and the values that are most important to you, such as integrity, creativity, or teamwork. These elements form the foundation of your brand, and understanding them will help you maintain consistency in everything you do.
- Be someone others can rely on. Follow through on your commitments, meet deadlines, and deliver quality work. Consistency in your actions and behavior builds trust and ensures people remember you.
- To stay relevant, learn new skills and stay updated on industry trends. This can mean taking new courses, attending workshops, or simply reading about the latest developments. This shows you are adaptable and always adding value.
- Share what you've achieved through presentations, reports, or even casual conversations with colleagues and managers. If others see your results and contributions, they'll associate you with that quality.
- Mentoring and sharing your knowledge with others helps you amplify your brand. Try to share your knowledge with others. If the information is not

confidential, you can write articles and blogs and participate in industry events.

- There's a balance between sharing your achievements and seeming arrogant. Find subtle ways to promote yourself, such as mentioning projects in meetings, updating your online profiles, or writing articles related to your field.
- Over time, your brand will grow stronger if you stay true to what you've defined as your strengths and values. If you change jobs, industries, or roles, adapt while keeping the core parts of your brand that make you unique.

Errors to Steer Clear of When Building Your Brand

Being Inauthentic: It's essential to be authentic and true to yourself. When your brand reflects who you are, it creates genuine connections. If you try to project a false image, people can usually tell, and that can hurt your credibility.

Over-Self-Promotion: While discussing your achievements or skills occasionally is great, doing so too often can seem self-focused. Instead, try to mix in some subtle self-promotion with a genuine interest in what others have to say—this approach usually works wonders. It's also wonderful when others share your excellent work.

Ignoring Feedback: Personal branding is all about how others perceive you, so embracing constructive criticism is crucial rather than ignoring it. By staying open to feedback and understanding how you're viewed, you can unlock valuable opportunities for growth and development.

Lacking Focus: Many individuals strive for perfection in all aspects, which can result in a fragmented personal brand. Trying to excel in various domains often obscures one's unique qualities. Instead, it's usually more effective to concentrate on a select few strengths that genuinely showcase one's distinguishing qualities.

Failing to Show Results: A brand that focuses solely on words without backing them up with actions tends to lack substance. To establish a trustworthy brand, it's vital to showcase genuine results and successes. Ensure your brand truly reflects your achievements and the positive impact you've made.

Not Maintaining the Brand: Personal branding necessitates consistent attention. Failing to maintain this—through continuous learning, networking, and remaining pertinent—may result in obsolescence. It is essential to persist in your efforts, even after establishing your brand.

In summary, a solid personal brand is crucial in today's job market, especially with the ongoing layoffs. It helps you stand out and creates new growth opportunities. When you consistently demonstrate your skills, values, and adaptability, others will see you as trustworthy and reliable, making you the preferred candidate for roles or projects. Additionally, a clear personal brand fosters meaningful relationships, which can lead to referrals and networking connections. Ultimately, your brand acts as both a safety net and a growth lever, giving you the confidence and resilience to navigate challenging job markets and positioning you as a valuable and adaptable professional.

<u>Exercise</u>

Task 1: Identify your brand and the value it provides. Consider situations in which others often seek your help and suggestions.

Task 2: Identify the areas of your personal brand and evaluate them against current market needs and industry standards to see if realignment is necessary.

Task 3: Evaluate the consistency of the brand you represent. Assess your consistency across actions and communications.

Task 4: Identify four tasks you will do over the next three months to further amplify your brand.

Section 2

CULTIVATING PERSONAL EXCELLENCE

This section is about the internal skills and traits that differentiate those who survive from those who thrive. You'll discover the power of emotional intelligence, mindfulness, and collaboration, learning how these personal attributes can make or break your career. By embracing continuous learning, nurturing strong relationships, and mastering your mindset, you'll develop the resilience to navigate the most demanding times with grace and confidence. These chapters will equip you to face uncertainty head-on, not just adapting to change but using it as a springboard to elevate your career. Learn to cultivate a growth mindset that propels you forward, no matter the challenges.

Chapter 7

Emotional Intelligence (EI) – Navigating People and Situations

In this chapter, we will discuss:

- The importance of emotional intelligence in the workplace.
- Strategy for integrating emotional intelligence into our everyday life.

Emotional intelligence (EI) involves understanding and managing our emotions while forming meaningful connections with others. It is a highly valuable skill in today's fast-paced work environment. With advancing technology, evolving work preferences, and the challenges of restructuring, workplaces have become more dynamic and unpredictable than ever. In this changing landscape, relying solely on technical skills is insufficient; it's essential to have strong emotional intelligence to adapt to changes, collaborate effectively with teammates, and recover from setbacks. Individuals with high emotional intelligence often manage stress gracefully, build stronger relationships, and leave lasting impressions, all of which can lead to exciting new opportunities. EI is crucial for continuous growth, helping us navigate uncertainty, stay motivated, and contribute meaningfully, even in tough times. Especially in service-oriented roles, emotional intelligence empowers professionals.

"Emotional intelligence (EI) is the ability to understand and manage emotions—both your own and those of others. It's a set of skills that helps you navigate relationships, handle stress, and make better decisions."

Recently, I had the opportunity to lead a major transformation project for a large service provider. The strategy lead was incredibly enthusiastic about this transformative journey. Soon after, my team began collaborating with various stakeholders and technology leads. However, we encountered a challenge when one individual from the customer side consistently questioned and challenged every suggestion we proposed. He would come into meetings and doubt my team's ability to execute the project. It caught me off guard, especially since everyone except for him was very supportive and praised our approach. I discussed this situation with the project manager, and we agreed it would benefit me to meet with him to understand his perspective. Although he initially declined our invitation for a meeting, he eventually decided to sit down with us. I wanted this conversation to take place in an informal setting, so I chatted at a nearby café.

During our conversation over coffee, he shared that he was originally the lead for formulating the technology transformation approach before his leadership decided to involve my company. He had already started creating a blueprint for it. He felt the new management was questioning his skills and contributions by involving outside consultants like me. Once I understood his concerns, it became clear what influenced his responses. At that moment, I consciously listened to his insights and asked engaging questions about his work, steering our discussion in a positive direction. I expressed my appreciation for his efforts and reassured him that we were not there to undermine his work but rather to provide support to enhance and build upon what he had already achieved.

Over the following meetings, we started building on his foundation and involved him in core discussions, valuing his input on critical decisions. Gradually, he began to appreciate our contributions and show us his support. We created a win-win outcome by understanding and addressing the emotional barriers in this situation. You will often hear management say they need skills beyond technical ones for senior roles. Emotional intelligence is highly valued in such situations, as you must interact with multiple stakeholders as you grow into senior levels.

The example I shared above is from an external project. It shows how crucial emotional intelligence can be when working with others. This applies to all our daily interactions at the office and at home. Emotional intelligence (EI) is a key ingredient for success in personal and professional settings.

Characteristics of Emotional Intelligence

Emotional intelligence in the context of corporate jobs is recognized for its significant impact on workplace dynamics and overall efficiency. It consists of five crucial characteristics.

Self-Awareness: Understanding oneself is vital to personal growth and emotional intelligence. It involves recognizing and comprehending your own emotions, strengths, weaknesses, values, and the impact you have on those around you. When individuals attain self-awareness, they become attuned to the specific triggers that elicit their emotions. For instance, situations or interactions that provoke frustration or joy can significantly influence how they behave or make decisions. Self-aware individuals not only reflect on their internal states but also acknowledge how these emotions shape their responses. This insight enhances personal well-being and fosters healthier relationships, as one can navigate social dynamics with greater empathy and understanding. Below are some simple steps you can take to boost your self-awareness:

- Spend a few minutes each day reflecting on how you felt and why. Write down moments that triggered strong emotions and consider what influenced those reactions.
- Ask trusted colleagues or friends how they perceive your reactions in different situations. This helps you see yourself from another perspective and identify areas for growth.
- Recognise situations that frequently evoke certain emotions, like frustration or joy, and examine what these patterns reveal about your underlying values or expectations.

Self-Regulation: Effectively managing your emotions and impulses is crucial for aligning your actions with your goals and values. It is a skill that entails maintaining a sense of calm, especially in challenging situations, and adapting gracefully to change. The ability to respond thoughtfully, rather than reacting impulsively, is a hallmark of strong self-regulation. Individuals who possess this skill can navigate stressful circumstances easily and comfortably, making them better equipped to deal with life's various challenges. One can enhance personal and professional relationships, improve decision-making, and foster overall well-being by cultivating self-regulation. Thus, developing this skill is essential for personal growth and achieving a fulfilling life. Here are some simple steps you can take to boost your self-regulation:

- When emotions are high, pause before responding. This can help you choose a measured response rather than an impulsive one.
- Techniques like deep breathing, meditation, or mindfulness exercises can help you stay calm under pressure.
- Instead of dwelling on what went wrong, focus on finding solutions. This will keep you productive and positively engaged.

Intrinsic Motivation: Individuals with a strong inner drive possess a remarkable ability to pursue their goals with both energy and unwavering persistence. This intrinsic motivation often propels them to strive for success despite minimal external rewards. Emotionally intelligent people exemplify this trait; they tend to be self-motivated and maintain an optimistic outlook, even in the face of challenges and setbacks. Their ability to stay positive not only helps them overcome obstacles but also fuels their resilience. This resilience is essential, as it enables these individuals to remain focused on their long-term objectives, allowing them to achieve sustained success over time. In essence, their inner drive acts as a guiding force, pushing them to persevere and thrive regardless of the circumstances they encounter. Here are some simple actions you can take to boost your intrinsic motivation:

- Define clear personal and professional goals that align with your values. Motivation increases when your work has meaning and purpose.
- Recognise and celebrate your achievements, no matter how small. Acknowledging progress keeps motivation high and reinforces resilience.
- View challenges as learning opportunities rather than obstacles. This mindset fuels motivation by valuing improvement over perfection.

Empathy: Empathy is such an important part of emotional intelligence. It's all about understanding and truly appreciating the emotions, perspectives, and concerns of others. It goes beyond just noticing; empathy encourages us to actively respond to the needs of those around us. When we foster empathy, we improve our communication skills and build deeper connections with others. Whether in our personal lives or at work, this emotional intelligence is key to creating stronger and more trusting relationships. When people feel understood and valued, they open up and communicate honestly, which helps us work together more effectively. In leadership, empathy shines even brighter. Leaders who practice empathy cultivate a supportive work environment where team members feel safe sharing their thoughts and feelings. This not only lifts morale but also boosts productivity, as people are more inclined to take initiative and share their creative ideas when they know their viewpoints are acknowledged and respected. Ultimately, empathy enriches our interpersonal relationships and is vital to effective leadership, helping create a collaborative and high-performing culture. Here are some simple actions you can take to boost your empathy:

- Practice active listening in every conversation. Show genuine interest, ask open-ended questions, and listen to understand rather than respond.
- Pay attention to body language, facial expressions, and tone of voice. These clues often reveal feelings beyond spoken words.
- When conflicts arise, try to understand the other person's perspective. This will help you respond more understandingly and constructively.

Social Skills: Building strong relationships, communicating effectively, and inspiring those around you are essential skills in our connected world. People with excellent social skills not only create valuable networks but also handle conflicts gracefully and nurture a sense of cooperation among diverse groups. Previously, I shared how important it is to forge connections, especially in professional settings, but these skills shine just as brightly in social interactions. As you enhance your social proficiency, you'll discover the ability to create positive bonds that enrich your life and significantly benefit those you engage with. Connecting meaningfully with others helps cultivate environments where collaboration flourishes, and mutual understanding becomes the norm. Ultimately, these invaluable skills pave the way for fulfilling relationships that support personal success and contribute to the overall well-being of our community. In the last chapter, we also revisited the significance of nurturing connections. Here are some simple steps you can take to boost your social skills.

- Be clear, concise, and open in your communication. Practice expressing yourself in ways that are positive and supportive.
- When conflicts arise, approach them calmly, listen to all perspectives, and focus on finding a solution that benefits everyone.
- Invest in building genuine relationships rather than just increasing the number of connections. Support others, celebrate their successes, and build trust through consistent, positive interactions.

Emotional intelligence is not something that develops instantly or without effort. It is a multifaceted skill set that requires consistent practice and self-awareness. Each day, look for opportunities to engage with the various components of emotional intelligence. For instance, you might show patience when interacting with a colleague, maintain your composure in a demanding meeting, or provide encouragement to someone who is struggling.

It's essential to take the time to reflect on how you responded to these scenarios. Ask yourself questions about your performance: What did you handle well? What could you improve upon? This reflective practice is crucial, allowing you to learn from your experiences and grow continuously. Regularly assessing your emotional responses and making the necessary adjustments will gradually enhance your emotional intelligence skills. Remember, mastery comes with persistence and a willingness to learn from every situation you encounter.

<u>Exercise</u>

Task 1: List five recent situations that sparked strong emotions (positive or negative), describe your reactions, and analyze why you responded that way. Consider if your response was constructive and aligned with your values.

Task 2: For at least the next four weeks, offer genuine appreciation or positive feedback to someone, whether a colleague, friend, or family member. Be specific about what you appreciate.

Task 3: For the next few days, practice pausing for 10 seconds when you feel strong emotions. Take deep breaths and consider your response. Ensure your reaction aligns with your desired outcome.

Task 4: During your next conversation, listen empathically. After they finish, summarize what they said in your own words to confirm your understanding.

Chapter 8

Collaborate, Not Compete – Thriving Together

In this chapter, we will discuss:

- Why collaboration is a critical skill in the corporate world.
- Approaches to strengthen collaboration under challenging scenarios.

Collaboration has become a central theme in today's professional landscape, and its significance cannot be overstated. While many of us are aware of its importance and occasionally engage in collaborative efforts, we often approach collaboration reactively—only reaching out to others when we feel overwhelmed or when a task seems insurmountable on our own. Yet, as we progress in our careers, we quickly discover that the capacity to work independently is limited.

The demands of our roles often extend well beyond our capabilities, pushing us into spaces where collaboration is beneficial and essential. We are expected to devise solutions that resonate with a larger audience, each member possessing unique viewpoints on the challenges and potential pathways forward. In these complex scenarios, tackling problems in isolation can lead to oversight. When one chooses to forge ahead solo, there is a significant risk of developing solutions that are, at best, partial. This approach fails to consider the broader context and can lead to misalignments—what may seem like a viable solution from one perspective can overlook critical elements essential to others. Consequently, isolated solutions will grapple with failure sooner or later, as they do not encompass the complete scope of the problem they aim to address.

Recognizing the limitations of solitary problem-solving, we begin to understand that true innovation and practical solutions arise from diverse insights and collaborative efforts. By embracing a culture of collaboration, we enhance our ability to tackle complex issues and foster an environment where every team member's input is valued. This leads to more robust and comprehensive solutions that stand the test of time. Therefore, the ability to collaborate effectively becomes not just a skill but a necessity for long-term success in any professional journey.

In many professional environments, a common phenomenon emerges: individuals begin competing with their peers, each vying to establish themselves as the best in a group. While this competitive spirit is often rooted in healthy ambition, it can quickly spiral into counterproductive behavior. Anyone within the group can initiate it, which may lead to a chain reaction whereby every team member becomes solely focused on their achievements. Unfortunately, this tendency often overshadows a crucial skill for senior professionals: collaboration.

Lack of Collaboration Causes Ongoing Disconnection

I recently attended a review meeting to evaluate the performance of a team of senior members. The goal was to identify candidates who were potential contenders for a fast-track path toward their next promotion. However, as we delved deeper into the assessments, it became clear that the members were entangled in a web of competition, each striving to demonstrate their personal excellence rather than fostering a cooperative environment.

Despite the vast potential that teamwork could harness, the group pursued its individual objectives. This realization prompted us to take a more personal approach, engaging in one-on-one conversations with the team members to uncover the root of this competitive culture. To our surprise, a common theme emerged in their responses: many expressed that "it is very difficult to collaborate with others."

This startling admission begs the question: why is collaboration perceived as a challenge among seasoned professionals? Perhaps it stems from the pressures of performance metrics, where individual accomplishments are highlighted, and the focus shifts from collective success to personal accolades. Thus, it is imperative to address this mindset, as true advancement in any organization lies not in competition but in cooperation. By fostering an environment where collaboration is not only encouraged but celebrated, teams can unlock unprecedented levels of innovation and productivity. The key lies in rekindling the spirit of teamwork, reminding individuals that together they can achieve far more than they ever could alone. Ultimately, the power of collaboration can lead to greater success for both the individual and the organization as a whole.

When you engage in non-cooperative behavior, it often begins with a tiny spark of frustration or disagreement. You might unconsciously label others as "difficult to work with," and this seemingly innocuous judgment can set off a chain reaction. Over time, this mindset can evolve into a more hostile stance, and you might even feel antagonistic toward those you once collaborated with, creating an atmosphere of hostility.

At first, your intention may simply be to avoid collaboration with someone you perceive as challenging. However, this avoidance can lead to informal groups or cliques forming. Before you know it, the team that once worked harmoniously can start to divide into factions, each group unified by their disdain for the other. This division hampers productivity and stifles the potential for creative solutions that often arise from diverse perspectives.

It's essential to remember that we are all human. Naturally, certain behaviors can be grating or disconcerting, provoking a strong response from us. However, rather than trying to change how others operate—an often futile endeavor—it's more beneficial to focus on adjusting your reactions and strategies. Embracing a mindset of understanding and flexibility can lead to more constructive interactions. This adaptability is particularly crucial for those in senior positions, where navigating complex team dynamics can enhance leadership effectiveness. As you cultivate positive relationships and demonstrate a collaborative spirit, you position yourself as a critical player within your organization and increase your chances of being retained during layoffs.

Furthermore, this proactive approach can significantly strengthen your resume, making you a more attractive candidate for future job opportunities. Instead of labeling colleagues as adversaries, seek to understand their motivations and viewpoints. Fostering an environment of collaboration rather than division can allow the entire team to thrive, allowing for a more productive and harmonious workplace. In essence, the power to change the dynamics of teamwork lies within your hands, primarily through your approach to such challenging interactions.

Changing the Definition of Collaboration

Collaboration is often perceived as a straightforward technique in which a group converges toward a shared consensus. Traditionally, the process involves selecting a leader, establishing guidelines, and collectively striving toward a common objective. However, in today's complex landscape, this conventional collaboration model is increasingly impractical. The notion that we can assemble diverse leaders into one room and emerge with a singular conclusion is a romanticized ideal that rarely plays out in practice.

Instead, we should reframe our understanding of collaboration. It is not merely about reaching a unanimous agreement; it is an opportunity to engage with a rich tapestry of perspectives, each contributing unique insights shaped by their distinct experiences. The true power of collaboration lies in the ability to acknowledge and discuss diverse problems, which leads to a flourishing of different viewpoints and multifaceted solutions.

For collaboration to be effective, you don't need to find common ground on every issue or agree on a singular path forward. The beauty of collaboration is rooted in this diversity. It unfolds through the sharing of ideas, the respectful exchange of opinions, and the exploration of various solutions, even when consensus eludes the group. Each discussion becomes a stepping stone, facilitating understanding and fostering innovation.

By embracing this broader interpretation of collaboration, we encourage a culture where divergent thoughts are welcomed and celebrated. We can harness the collective potential of diverse minds to navigate complicated challenges and inspire creative pathways forward. The essence of collaboration transforms from the pursuit of agreement to the discovery of understanding, allowing for a more inclusive and dynamic problem-solving process that reflects the complexities of our modern world.

Collaborating with Challenging Peers

In collaborating with challenging peers, it's essential to recognize that productive collaboration doesn't require complete agreement on every detail.

Agree to Disagree on Details: In any collaborative setting, it's crucial to acknowledge the diverse perspectives that individuals bring to the table. Each person possesses unique experiences, beliefs, and insights that shape how they perceive situations. Therefore, it's not uncommon for you and your peers to have differing viewpoints. However, what truly matters is our ability to focus on the broader vision we all strive to achieve. This approach is not about forcing agreement on every minor detail but about recognizing the inherent worth in each individual's perspective. When we commit to understanding one another, even amidst disagreement, we enhance our collaborative efforts and enrich our collective experiences.

Emphasize the Shared Vision: In any collaborative environment, it is essential to maintain a clear focus on the common goals and the overarching purpose of the team. This shared vision acts as a guiding star, illuminating the path forward, even when individual members bring diverse methods and opinions. When team members shift their attention from personal viewpoints to the shared objectives, they see each other not as opponents but as allies working toward a common goal. By embracing the team's core purpose and letting it guide interactions, you can create a productive workspace and a harmonious one where every voice matters in the grand symphony of collaboration.

Define Collaborative Zones: Identify areas where alignment is essential and others where individual approaches are acceptable. For example, if you are both responsible for separate tasks within a project, agree on deliverables and deadlines while allowing room for each person's style or approach.

Prioritize Respect over Agreement: Respect is a cornerstone of effective collaboration, playing a more pivotal role than simple agreement. When team members honor and acknowledge each other's viewpoints, they transcend mere positionality and enter a realm where understanding flourishes. This act of genuinely valuing another's perspective, regardless of individual beliefs or stances, fosters a culture of trust that becomes the bedrock of teamwork.

In such an environment, individuals feel safe to express their ideas and concerns without fear of judgment. This openness enhances communication and sparks creativity, as diverse thoughts are allowed to intermingle. The result is a collaboration that is not only more productive but also profoundly satisfying. When people collaborate in a climate of mutual respect, they discover that working together is not just a means to an end, but a shared journey toward collective success. And in this journey, the camaraderie built along the way turns the process into an enjoyable experience, where challenges are faced together, ideas are explored freely, and achievements are celebrated as a unified team. Ultimately, respect is not just a value; it's the very essence of a thriving collaborative spirit!

Commit to Flexibility: Being flexible and open to compromise allows us to appreciate both perspectives. It's great to occasionally consider your peers' ideas and encourage them to share theirs in return. This spirit of give-and-take fosters a collaborative relationship that thrives even without complete agreement.

Celebrate Progress, Not Perfection: In any collaborative endeavor, it is vital to focus on the milestones that we achieve together as a team rather than harboring unrealistic expectations of a perfectly smooth and conflict-free journey. The reality of working with others is that disagreements and challenges will surface; they are an intrinsic part of any group dynamic.

By acknowledging and celebrating our accomplishments, no matter how small, we cultivate a positive spirit of collaboration. This recognition serves as a morale booster, reminding us of our shared purpose and the progress made. Even when tensions arise, recognizing joint successes fosters a sense of unity. It encourages us to navigate conflicts with a problem-solving mindset instead of becoming mired in negativity.

In summary, collaborating with our peers, rather than competing, is vital for our growth, especially during tough organizational transitions. When we work together, we create a supportive network that helps us tackle challenges collectively and build strong professional relationships, essential for stability and resilience. Collaboration lets us share knowledge, foster trust, and develop a positive reputation, making us more adaptable and appreciated within the organization. By uniting with our peers and contributing to the team's success, we enhance our impact and ensure our growth remains steady, even in challenging work environments.

<u>Exercise</u>

Task 1: List the scenarios from your daily work where you find it challenging to collaborate with a peer.

Task 2: Analyze which behavior from others prompts you to say, "It's difficult or impossible to work with a specific person."

Task 3: Consider the steps you could take after reading this chapter to enhance collaboration.

Task 4: Identify and list some actions you would like to include in your subsequent collaborative work with peers.

CHAPTER 9

Mentoring – Building Success by Lifting Others

In this chapter, we will discuss:

- The importance of mentoring.
- Enhancing influence through effective mentoring.

In recent years, I encountered a phrase that profoundly shifted my understanding of personal and professional growth: "A true leader creates many more leaders like him or her." This simple yet powerful statement encapsulates the essence of effective leadership and the critical role of mentoring.

Mentoring is not merely a function of imparting knowledge; it is a compelling relationship that fosters mutual growth and development. One consistent piece of feedback I have received from the mentors in my life highlights the importance of helping others succeed. Celebrating their achievements is integral to this process. For mentors, recognizing the successes of their mentees is not only rewarding for the individuals being guided but also enhances the mentor's reputation in their field. Mentoring is inherently a two-way communication process. As a mentor, I have discovered that I, too, learn invaluable lessons from my mentees. Each individual possesses unique qualities and perspectives that can enrich our understanding of the world. This reciprocal dynamic reinforces the belief that learning is a lifelong endeavor;

we are all both mentors and mentees at different times in our lives and careers.

Take, for instance, my journey in writing this book. As I endeavor to share my insights and experiences, I am also supported by a network of mentors who guide me through this process. Simultaneously, I take pride in mentoring others in the industry. Participating in mentorship programs allows me to contribute to the development of future leaders while also gleaning fresh perspectives from each interaction.

In my recent mentoring session, I had the pleasure of engaging with a newly promoted team member. As we discussed his transition into this elevated role, he inquired about the additional responsibilities he should embrace as a senior member. He was clearly eager to grow and make a meaningful impact within our organization. One of the vital suggestions I offered was the importance of mentoring and guiding others. In any professional setting, the ability to contribute to the development of your colleagues is not just a noble endeavor but also a strategic approach to personal growth. While it's commendable to excel in your responsibilities, actual influence comes from the ability to empower those around you.

Indeed, you can leverage your unique skills and talents to make a difference, but there's a ceiling to how much impact you can have working in isolation. The most effective way to expand your influence is to cultivate a culture of mentorship. By mentoring others, you not only foster their growth but also amplify your impact exponentially—essentially creating 'copies' of yourself who are equipped to carry forward the organisation's vision and mission. As individuals ascend to higher levels within their organizations, there is an underlying expectation that they will perform their jobs to the best of their abilities. However, many professionals find themselves at a crossroads, delivering exceptional results within their roles yet struggling to find avenues for broader contribution. They become ensnared in the day-to-day functions of their positions, inadvertently limiting their potential.

To break free from this stagnation, one of the simplest yet most effective pathways is through mentoring. By dedicating time to mentor others, seasoned professionals can foster an environment of growth, collaboration, and shared success. This not only enhances the capabilities of the team but also enriches the mentor's own skill set and understanding of their field. Ultimately, through nurturing talent and developing the next generation of leaders, we not only fulfill our organizational obligations but also leave a lasting legacy that resonates far beyond our personal achievements.

Mentoring Benefits Everyone

Mentoring others can be a profound and transformative experience, both for the mentor and the mentee. One of the most common hesitations many individuals face when considering the role of a mentor is the fear of sharing their knowledge. The concern often lies in the belief that by imparting what they know, they might diminish their own value or expertise. However, this perception couldn't be further from the truth. In fact, mentoring others can significantly elevate your own value in both personal and professional contexts. When you mentor someone, you not only share your knowledge but also open doors to new collaborations and experiences that you may have never anticipated. It creates a fertile ground for innovative ideas to flourish.

For instance, I had the opportunity to mentor a mentee who came from a completely different domain, country, and culture. This diversity brought a fresh perspective to our discussions, leading us to uncover a plethora of new opportunities for collaboration. Together, we embarked on various inventive projects that culminated in numerous patents. The process involved introducing her to the concept of invention and guiding her to channel her energy effectively. As we brainstormed and innovated, the results were beneficial for both of us. What began as a series of mentoring sessions blossomed into a creative partnership that resulted in new products and features—outcomes that we both celebrated with pride.

Mentoring others transcends mere skill; it is an essential pillar for survival and growth in today's tumultuous industry landscape, which is often marked by layoffs and a scarcity of job opportunities. Amidst such uncertainty, those who take on mentoring roles not only showcase their leadership abilities but also distinguish themselves in the eyes of their peers and superiors.

At its core, mentoring is about more than just guidance; it's about fostering a network of trust and mutual respect. When mentors actively invest time and energy into the development of others, they pave the way for new opportunities—not only for their mentees but also for themselves—as they establish invaluable connections within the organization. These relationships can lead to collaborations, partnerships, and even friendships that are vital in navigating the complexities of a challenging work environment. Mentoring creates a ripple effect, fostering a culture of growth and resilience within organizations. It encourages a proactive approach to personal and professional development, empowering individuals to take charge of their careers, even amidst adversity. As mentors and mentees navigate this journey together, they build not just skills but a legacy of support and inspiration that can uplift entire teams, leading to sustained success in an ever-evolving industry landscape.

Moreover, mentors develop a deeper understanding of their own expertise, as teaching often brings new insights and reinforces one's knowledge. In industries with fewer opportunities, mentors create a legacy of value and support within the organization, showing that they contribute not just to individual projects but to the growth of the entire team. This influence can solidify their role as indispensable members of the company, making them more resilient during times of change. Mentorship cultivates a reputation for adaptability, value, and commitment to team success, positioning mentors as leaders who can thrive regardless of industry challenges.

Traits of a Good Mentor:

Everyone has room for improvement, and we all have the chance to grow into an even better version of ourselves. Here are some wonderful approaches you can consider to become a truly great mentor:

Be Genuinely Invested: Show a sincere interest in your mentees' growth and goals. When you are truly invested in their success, they can easily sense your commitment. This fosters trust and encourages a supportive relationship.

Listen Actively: Great mentors truly excel at listening. Be sure to carve out time for your mentees, really hear their concerns, and create a space where they feel comfortable sharing openly. By practicing active listening, you'll gain a deeper understanding of their needs, allowing you to offer more personalized guidance effectively.

Share Knowledge Generously: Feel free to share your insights, experiences, and resources. When you open up with your expertise, you become a trusted go-to for valuable information, boosting your reputation as a knowledgeable and helpful resource mentor.

Provide Constructive Feedback: Provide sincere, constructive feedback that facilitates mentee growth, avoiding excessive criticism. By offering your insights in a kind and practical manner, mentees are more inclined to value your guidance and recognize you as someone who truly wishes to support their development and growth.

Encourage Independence: Great mentors play a vital role in helping their mentees become self-sufficient. By encouraging critical thinking, problem-solving, and decision-making, you foster a sense of independence that shows your belief in their potential. This boosts their confidence and strengthens your reputation as a mentor who empowers others without the need to micromanage.

Celebrate Their Success: Take a moment to recognize and celebrate the amazing achievements of your mentees. When others observe your genuine pride in their accomplishments, it reinforces your reputation as a mentor who deeply cares about the success of others.

Model Positive Values and Behavior: Your actions truly make a difference. By demonstrating integrity, respect, and a positive attitude in your work, you inspire your mentees to follow your example. Being a role model in values and behavior not only enhances your mentoring but also creates a supportive environment for everyone involved in reputation.

Continuously Improve Your Mentoring Skills: It's so helpful to seek feedback from your mentees and others.

By actively working on your mentoring skills, you show humility and a genuine commitment to personal growth, which are wonderful qualities that can truly enhance your reputation.

Can I have Multiple Mentors?

One of the most frequently asked questions I encounter is whether it's acceptable to have multiple mentors. The answer is a resounding yes! Embracing the idea of having several mentors can be one of the most empowering decisions you make in your personal and professional journey. Having diverse mentors allows you to tap into a wealth of perspectives and insights that can greatly enrich your growth. Each mentor brings their unique expertise, experiences, and viewpoints, which can foster a more rounded understanding of your field or interests. Consider, for instance, a mentor who excels in technical knowledge, another who is a proven leader, and yet another who specializes in personal development. This eclectic mix can provide a robust foundation that supports your multifaceted journey.

However, it's vital to approach this mentoring relationship with thoughtfulness and intentionality. Start by identifying specific areas where you seek growth and look for mentors who align with those goals. Remember, it's not merely about accumulating mentors; it's about forging meaningful and productive relationships. Mindfulness regarding their time is crucial; ensure that you respect their boundaries and commitments. Acknowledge that they are giving you their valuable time and insights, so being considerate is important. Moreover, maintaining clarity regarding your objectives with each mentor is fundamental. This means being transparent about what you hope to learn and ensuring that there's no overlap that could lead to confusion. Open communication is key here; don't hesitate to discuss your goals and how you envision the mentoring relationship. By articulating your aspirations and being receptive to the guidance offered, you create a safe space for constructive dialogue. As you navigate the advice and insights you receive, remain flexible and open to adaptation. Each mentor may offer differing perspectives or suggestions—embrace this diversity as an opportunity for growth. The ability to synthesize various pieces of advice can enhance your decision-making skills and, ultimately, your development.

In summary, In a world marked by change and adversity, mentoring creates a mutually beneficial cycle that nurtures resilience, adaptability, and long-term success for everyone involved. A mentor helps you navigate uncertainty, providing valuable insights that foster personal and professional growth. Equally important is stepping into the role of a mentor for others—by sharing your knowledge and experiences, you not only contribute to their development but also strengthen your own leadership and problem-solving skills.

<u>Exercise</u>

Task 1: Identify your weak areas where you need mentorship.

Task 2: Identify your strong areas where you can act as a mentor.

Task 3: Note the impact of your mentorship on your mentee and organisation.

Task 4: Identify which skills you need to improve to become a good mentor.

Chapter 10

Lifelong Learning – Your Key to Staying Relevant

In this chapter, we will discuss:

- How continuous learning is a way to grow.
- Techniques to acquire new skills in a systematic manner.

Technology is evolving at an unprecedented pace, reshaping the world we inhabit every day. As we strive to master one facet of innovation, it seems that another breakthrough materializes, often before we fully grasp the implications of the last. Each year introduces a new buzzword into our lexicon, capturing the imagination of entrepreneurs and consumers alike. In the initial chapters of this book, I discussed how companies are continuously adapting to these rapid technological shifts to maintain their competitive edge and profitability. Some businesses leverage these emerging technologies to enhance their profit margins, innovating by providing new services and products that cater to evolving consumer demands. As companies expand their capabilities and workforce, this often results in the creation of new job roles. Conversely, some organizations view these advancements primarily through the lens of cost reduction. They implement automation and artificial intelligence as strategies to streamline operations and minimize expenses, typically at the expense of human jobs.

For instance, I recently worked with a major multinational corporation (MNC) that aimed to reduce its workforce in a specific department by 25% over the next few years. Their strategy involved adopting automation and AI technologies to replace traditional roles, arguing that these solutions are more efficient, reliable, and faster than human labor. This shift reveals a critical dynamic in the current technological landscape: these innovations are akin to double-edged swords. On the one hand, they foster the creation of new opportunities, potentially sparking entire industries; on the other hand, they inevitably lead to job losses, casting a shadow on the livelihoods of many employees.

Why Continuous Learning?

In our rapidly evolving landscape, embracing a continuous learning approach is essential as it fosters a culture that empowers everyone to navigate the complexities of new technologies and their impacts. This philosophy transcends technical teams; it is imperative for individuals in every department—from Management to Sales, Service, and Product Engineering—to engage in this exploration. Understanding how emerging technologies intersect with our respective fields cannot be overstated. Continuous learning is a powerful strategy for resilience in the changing job market for the following reasons:

- Regular learning helps you stay flexible with new technologies, processes, and changes in the industry. This flexibility makes it much easier to transition into new roles, adapt to organizational shifts, and embrace exciting job opportunities that call for the skills you've been honing.
- Employers see employees who actively pursue skill growth as even more valuable. Those who keep

developing relevant skills open themselves up to better opportunities, helping them maintain their current roles or smoothly transition to new ones as they align with the changing needs of their organizations.

- As the job landscape evolves and automation increases, especially for roles centred around routine tasks, it's a wonderful opportunity to learn and grow. By developing skills that automation can't easily replicate, such as critical thinking, emotional intelligence, and strategic decision-making, you'll set yourself up for success and stay valuable in the ever-changing workforce.

- If your current field is on a downward trend, embracing continuous learning can open up exciting opportunities for you to transition into a new and more stable industry. This approach not only expands your horizons but also allows you to harness your skills in various fields, giving you the freedom to explore different career paths.

- Employers and recruiters appreciate when individuals commit to personal growth. By consistently learning new skills, you cultivate a strong personal brand that reflects resilience, ambition, and forward-thinking. This enhances your profile and makes you a standout candidate in a competitive job market!

- It's reassuring to realise that by actively preparing for upcoming changes, you're developing a strong sense of control, which helps alleviate concerns regarding job loss or unexpected shifts in the industry. Furthermore, trusting your capacity to swiftly acquire new skills significantly diminishes worries about becoming outdated.

- At times, the position you aspire to or the role required by your organisation has not yet been established. Engaging in continuous learning equips you to transition into these developing roles, providing you with an advantage over others who may find it challenging to adapt.

Skill Concepts

Reflecting on the past few years, we initially championed the concept of T-shaped skills. This model emphasized having a primary area of expertise while maintaining a broad understanding of other relevant skills in our industry. However, as we advanced, we transitioned towards Pi-shaped skills, whereby professionals are expected to excel in two core disciplines while still being knowledgeable about additional areas.

Yet, as we delve deeper into the realm of technological advancement, it becomes evident that even the Pi-shaped skills may soon feel antiquated. In a world where new technologies emerge increasingly, there simply isn't enough time to cultivate deep expertise in multiple areas. This observation leads us to a new model of comb-shaped skills.

A person possessing a comb-shaped skill set has several profound areas of expertise (akin to the "teeth" of a comb) along with a wide-ranging general knowledge in various fields. This method enables individuals to navigate complex, multidisciplinary environments effectively, making it particularly beneficial for roles that necessitate integration across diverse domains, such as consulting, product management, or interdisciplinary research. More teeth/skills need to be added as new areas of technology are emerging. At this point, you have two options — Make the comb denser by quickly learning adjacent technologies or add new skills, as shown in Image 1.

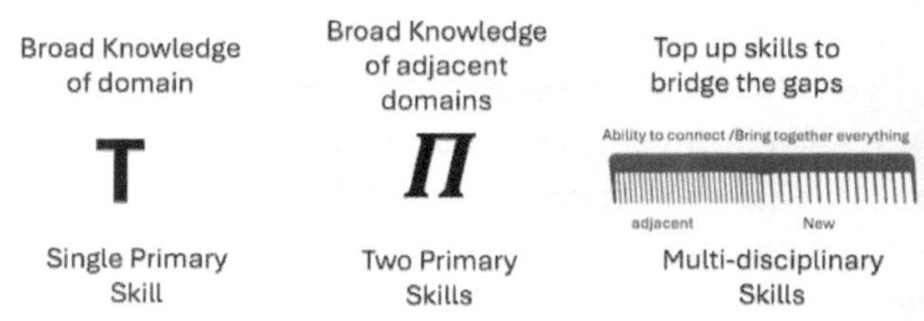

Image 1 – Skill Concepts

The dynamic approach presented by comb-shaped skills allows professionals to weave their competencies together, facilitating a deeper alignment with market needs. The comb-shaped skills framework not only allows for a robust skill set but also fosters resilience in the face of continual change. As you add layers to your foundational skills, this comb takes on a life of its own, growing larger and stronger, equipping you to thrive amidst the ever-changing technological landscape. The ongoing journey of learning and adaptation becomes not just a personal endeavor, but a collective hallmark of success in our fast-paced world.

Assess Your Skills and Market Relevance

Many individuals dive into learning new things without considering their fit with their organization or personal goals. Before starting any new learning endeavors, it's essential to evaluate your skills and market relevance. This self-assessment enables you to use your time and energy effectively, focusing on developing competencies that boost your employability and align with your long-term career aspirations.

Imagine standing at a crossroads where different paths represent various skills you can pursue. Before choosing a direction, it's vital to evaluate where you currently stand. By identifying specific skill gaps, you shed light on what you lack and what is necessary for advancement. Moreover, understanding industry trends is akin to having a map that guides you through the maze of professional development. These trends inform you about which skills are in high demand, helping you make informed decisions that align your learning journey with the current and future needs of the job market.

Engaging in this targeted approach empowers you to sidestep the pitfalls of acquiring outdated skills that may soon wane in relevance. Instead, you focus on learning that is pertinent and strategically essential for your growth. This foresight fosters a mindset of continuous improvement and adaptability; as the market evolves, so do your capabilities and roles.

Furthermore, this process of targeted learning serves as a powerful motivator. Each new skill acquired becomes a stepping stone toward your career goals, providing you with a clear sense of purpose. When you understand how each learning endeavor fits into the larger picture of your career trajectory, the process becomes not just an academic exercise but a transformative journey.

Ultimately, this approach positions you as a competitive and adaptable candidate in a fast-evolving job market. You become someone who does not merely react to changes but proactively shapes your career narrative. In a world where employers seek versatility and innovation, your commitment to continuous, relevant skill development sets you apart, making you an invaluable asset in any professional setting. So, the next question is, where to start?

How to Add New Teeth to a Comb

After identifying the skills you need to acquire, many of us feel it is a mammoth task. The challenge lies in figuring out how to begin developing these skills. Many of my mentees often ask me, "How do I start building a specific skill?" You may feel short on time or lacking the motivation to embark on a new learning journey. I want to share a straightforward technique my teacher introduced to me during my school days. It has consistently been effective for me and all my mentees who have embraced it. My teacher used to call this the packet system.

Step 1: Identify the topic you want to learn (don't think about the difficulty; you have to start somewhere).

Step 2: Begin gradually and allocate at least 20 minutes daily for that topic.

Step 3: Read, experiment, or discuss that topic for at least 20 minutes, and then daily summarize your learning as if you are explaining it to someone else in 2 minutes. Your learning becomes the packet, and the summary acts as a label. For me, summarizing with closed eyes at bedtime works best.

Step 4: The next day, learn for 20 minutes again and then summarize the previous day's learning along with the new learning from today. It's like putting more content in the packet and sealing it again.

Step 5: When you complete a week, start summarizing for each week, and it will create a weekly packet.

If you stick with this for just a few weeks, you'll notice how much you've learned about the topic without feeling like you've worked too hard. Staying consistent and taking summary notes are indeed the keys to making this approach work. Equally important is the practice of sharing your newfound knowledge with others. Reflecting on the ideas presented in the previous chapter, teaching what you've learned reinforces your understanding and develops your interpersonal skills. As you explain complex concepts to your peers, you bolster your grasp of the subject while enhancing your reputation as a reliable source of information. This is a crucial step in your journey because you inherently elevate your position within your field as you become a go-to person for answers.

As more individuals seek your expertise and your problem-solving capabilities grow, you find yourself progressing toward proficiency. What began as a simple packet of information—a tiny seed of knowledge—transforms into a factory of insights, where you are no longer just a learner but an owner of a vast reservoir of understanding. Each query you handle and every challenge you solve adds to your growing expertise. Essentially, you evolve from being just a student, absorbing knowledge, to becoming a knowledgeable mentor, guiding others through their journeys. Therefore, embrace this process wholeheartedly; it is rewarding and essential for your development as a skilled professional. You need to identify and focus on upcoming skills early. It's all about demand and supply. No one will be an expert in new technology at first; everyone will be experimenting. However, those who are consistent in learning and sharing will soon earn the title of expert.

In summary, continuous learning is paramount for both survival and success within the contemporary and challenging job market. As industries undergo rapid transformations due to technological advancements and changing demands, the consistent updating of skills enables professionals to maintain relevance, adaptability, and competitiveness. By dedicating oneself to lifelong learning, individuals can promptly respond to evolving circumstances, transition into new roles, and address any potential skill gaps. This proactive approach not only bolsters job security and marketability but also introduces opportunities for growth within emerging fields, empowering individuals to not merely survive but to actively shape their careers during uncertain times.

<u>Exercise</u>

Task 1: Assess your skills and knowledge to identify strengths and gaps, including technical and soft skills.

Task 2: List opportunities you will lose if you do not acquire the skills identified in the gap analysis.

Task 3: Based on your self-assessment and market research, set specific, measurable goals for skill development. Focus on skills that align with your career aspirations and market needs, creating short-term and long-term objectives.

Task 4: Find the best resources for each goal, such as online courses, workshops, or mentorship, and establish a regular learning routine.

Chapter 11

Mindfulness at Work – Finding Calm Amidst Chaos

In this chapter, we will discuss:

- Techniques to focus on critical items.
- The art of detachment.

In the previous chapter, I delved into the importance of continuous learning, particularly in our fast-paced and ever-evolving world. Organizations today are not merely looking for employees who are good at their specific tasks; they seek individuals equipped with multidisciplinary skills that enable them to adapt, innovate, and thrive in diverse environments.

However, a significant challenge arises in this pursuit of knowledge: the overwhelming abundance of information and skills available to us. When faced with the seemingly endless list of competencies to master, it is easy to become paralyzed by choice. We often struggle to juggle multiple projects and learning objectives simultaneously, leading to confusion and a sense of being stretched too thin.

To illustrate this point, I reflect on a recent conversation with one of my mentees. He was initially enthusiastic about developing a single skill, setting out a plan to dedicate the next month to becoming proficient in that area. This commitment was a wise move, aimed at fostering depth before attempting to cover more ground. Yet, as he engaged with peers and was inundated by various buzzwords and emerging trends, he felt the urge to expand his focus. Before long, he shifted his attention to many endeavors at once. What was the outcome of this relentless pursuit of knowledge? At the end of the month, rather than the anticipated progress, my mentee found himself more confused than ever. His earlier clarity had dissipated, and he had made little tangible advancement in any skills he had attempted to learn.

This experience highlights a crucial lesson: While enthusiasm for learning is commendable, it is essential to maintain focus and avoid the trap of dispersion. In an age of abundant information and options, it is vital to prioritize, concentrate on one goal at a time, and ensure that our learning efforts yield meaningful results. Only then can we truly harness the potential of continuous learning to enhance our skills and advance in our careers.

Are We Really Multitasking?

Multitasking is a term we frequently hear in our fast-paced world, often touted as an essential skill for success in both personal and professional realms. However, let's take a moment to delve deeper into the nature of multitasking. We must recognize a fundamental truth: even when we appear to be juggling multiple responsibilities simultaneously, our brains can only focus on one task at a time. This is rooted in our cognitive architecture; human brains are not inherently designed for true parallel processing. When engaged in what we perceive as multitasking, we merely switch between tasks, which can lead to inefficiencies and decreased overall productivity. Each time we transition from one task to another, there is a brief moment of mental adjustment that can detract from our effectiveness and from the quality of our work. Hence, while it may feel as if we are handling many tasks at once, we often find ourselves merely skimming the surface of each rather than diving deeply into any single one.

Given this reality, it becomes crucial to prioritize what truly matters in our lives and careers. By focusing our efforts and dedicating uninterrupted time to each task or learning opportunity, we can achieve a higher level of engagement and a deeper understanding of our work. This approach enhances the quality of our output and fosters greater satisfaction and a sense of accomplishment. Ultimately, actual productivity lies in recognizing the limits of our cognitive abilities and making conscious choices to allocate our time and energy where it will have the most significant impact. While multitasking is often glamorized in today's society, understanding and embracing the advantages of focused effort is critical to achieving meaningful results. It's time to reconsider our approaches and techniques, allowing for dedicated time to fully immerse ourselves in each task.

Organizations and their leaders continually strive to achieve favorable outcomes that align closely with their company objectives. However, there is a tendency for individuals within these organizations to become overwhelmed by taking on an excessive number of tasks. This phenomenon can lead to a paradox where, instead of enhancing productivity and performance, the result is often a decline in the quality of work delivered.

It is common for many employees to volunteer for numerous projects, raising their hands to participate in various initiatives, yet becoming burdened by the sheer volume of responsibilities. This scenario is detrimental not only to the organisation but also negatively impacts the employees themselves. When stretched too thin, individuals struggle to meet the expectations or requirements of any task, leading to frustration and reduced efficiency.

To counteract this challenge, it is crucial to adopt a more strategic approach to work. Identify activities where you can make a wider impact based on your skills. Secondly, when faced with multiple tasks, consider dedicating specific time slots to each responsibility. This means deliberately setting aside uninterrupted periods where one can focus solely on a single task at hand. By minimizing distractions and prioritizing attention, employees are more likely to deliver exceptional results, thus contributing to the organisation's overall success and ensuring that their efforts are both meaningful and impactful.

The Art of Detachment

Mastering certain techniques can lead to substantial improvements in our personal and professional lives. One such technique that I have found particularly transformative is the art of detachment. While often overlooked, this concept holds the key to navigating the complexities of our daily routines with grace and effectiveness.

I have repeatedly witnessed the remarkable outcomes of practicing detachment throughout my journey. Friends, colleagues, and mentees frequently inquire about my ability to juggle various responsibilities – from managing a demanding job and innovating novel ideas to attending industry events and nurturing family connections. The secret lies not in the frantic rush to accomplish everything but rather in how we approach these tasks.

Our minds tend to wander in the hustle and bustle of our modern lives. This seemingly innocuous phenomenon can become a significant barrier to our productivity and presence at the moment. Our thoughts frequently drift toward those facets of existence that lie beyond our control. It is common for individuals to reflect on past events or indulge in daydreams about an uncertain future. While introspection about our past and aspirations for the future can possess their value, we must cultivate the ability to keep our minds calm and focused on the present task at hand.

I recently came across a thought-provoking YouTube video featuring a student addressing his teacher with a relatable concern. Despite his efforts to concentrate, his mind incessantly recalled snippets of music he had heard earlier in the day. This scenario highlights the challenge of mental distractions that many of us face. In response to the student's query, the teacher imparted a simple yet profound solution: when attempting to maintain focus, try listening to instrumental music instead of songs with lyrics. The rationale behind this advice is intriguing; by selecting instrumental tracks, the brain is less likely to seize upon verbal cues and remain less distracted by the urge to engage with the lyrics. While I cannot definitively claim that this technique has worked wonders for the student, I, too, have used gentle natural sounds to avoid distraction in a noisy environment. You can easily find them on YouTube or other streaming platforms under the focus music category. In essence, it's about harnessing our focus and making mindful choices that nurture our mental clarity, steering us away from the internal and external noise that can so quickly derail our efforts to be present.

Detachment does not imply disinterest or an absence of commitment. Instead, it cultivates a mindset that allows us to engage fully with each activity while maintaining a healthy distance from the stress and pressures often accompanying them. By mastering the art of detachment, we can focus on the present moment and make decisions that reflect our true priorities without being overwhelmed by the noise of external expectations.

Thus, in understanding this technique, I encourage you to explore it more deeply. Consider how detachment can elevate your life, allowing you to find balance amidst the chaos and ultimately achieve remarkable results both personally and professionally. Embracing this approach may very well be the key to unlocking your full potential, enabling you to thrive while managing the diverse facets of life with ease and clarity. Some of the techniques you can use to practice the art of detachment include:

Mindfulness Practices: Start by spending five minutes a day focusing on your breathing, tuning into how your body feels, or simply observing the beauty around you. This little practice can truly help anchor you in the present moment.

Label your thoughts and let them go. When a thought about the past or future sneaks in, label it as "past" or "future" and gently remind yourself to release it. Redirect your attention back to the now without any judgment. This nurturing approach builds a wonderful habit of letting go of unhelpful thinking.

Set Clear Intentions: Each morning, take a moment to jot down three things you'd like to focus on that are within your control. This simple act can help clear away mental clutter by guiding your mind toward what you can actively influence and achieve.

Establish "Worry Times": Designate a special time, like 10 minutes a day, to ponder your worries. If worries pop up outside of that time, kindly remind yourself that they can wait until then. This helpful practice allows you to compartmentalize your concerns and feel a bit lighter.

Break Tasks Into Steps: If you feel overwhelmed, try breaking tasks down into small, manageable steps you can take one at a time. This strategy helps you focus your mind and direct your energy toward what you can do right now.

Practice Gratitude: Each day, write down a few things you're thankful for. This lovely habit can train your brain to notice the wonderful positives in the present instead of getting caught up in the negatives.

During challenging times, focusing on what you can control can really uplift your productivity, adaptability, and resilience—all important qualities for advancing your career. By practicing mindfulness and using present-focused techniques, you can cut down on distractions and stress. This helps you learn quickly, excel under pressure, and utilize your resources wisely. With this approach, you'll be able to create meaningful results, foster a positive reputation, and enhance your skills, making you a valuable and adaptable team player who shines, even in the face of layoffs or restructuring. By consistently using these strategies, you not only thrive but also set yourself up for greater opportunities, no matter what uncertainties come your way!

<u>Exercise</u>

Task 1: Write down worries and identify what's within your control, set a dedicated time and action to address them.

Task 2: Prioritize your tasks and identify them for immediate execution, delegation, or elimination.

Task 3: Choose one activity daily to do with full, undivided attention.

Task 4: Set a daily reminder to pause and list three things you're grateful for in that moment.

Chapter 12

Navigating the Unknown – Dealing with Ambiguity

In this chapter, we will discuss:

- Strategies to deal with the fear of the unknown.
- Mental preparedness with Plan B.

In this book, I have consistently emphasized the rapidly evolving landscape of technology and consumer behavior and their profound impact on jobs and the skills required for the modern workforce. The pace of technological advancements is staggering; new technologies emerge and gain popularity within mere weeks, fundamentally altering the way we work and live. Historically, organizations were hesitant to embrace anything other than well-established, mature technologies and solutions. This cautious approach was largely due to the inherent risks associated with adopting untested innovations. However, a significant shift has occurred in recent years. Companies are now eager to integrate these emerging technologies into their operations at the earliest opportunity, recognizing that being an early adopter can provide a competitive edge in today's fast-paced market.

I recall a conversation with a sales professional who perfectly captured the essence of this new mindset. He remarked, "I should have earned that dollar yesterday." This statement encapsulates the urgency with which businesses are now operating; the pressure to stay ahead of the curve has never been greater. Those who fail to adapt risk falling behind as the velocity of change continues to accelerate.

The implications of these developments extend far beyond just technology adoption. They challenge traditional notions of job security and the types of skills that will be in demand. As businesses pivot rapidly to harness the power of new tools and technologies, there is an increasing need for a workforce that is agile, adaptable, and continuously learning. In this context, the importance of lifelong learning and professional development cannot be overstated, as individuals strive to keep pace with the shifting demands of their industries.

Fear of Unknown

Fear of the unknown is a universal experience, one that can grip individuals at any stage of life or in any circumstance. It's important to recognize that this fear is a natural response to uncertainty and can often feel overwhelming. However, there is a powerful strategy to combat this trepidation: preparation.

The best way to tackle the fear of the unknown is to prepare for the worst. This may sound counterintuitive—after all, why focus on adverse outcomes when one can foster positivity? But acknowledging the possibility of adverse scenarios allows us to mentally and emotionally brace ourselves. By contemplating and developing a plan B, we not only equip ourselves with tools and strategies to handle potential challenges but also diminish the power that fear holds over us. When we have a contingency plan in place, we cultivate a sense of control amidst chaos. This approach does not mean that we should dwell on negativity or live in a state of anxiety; instead, it encourages us to face our fears with clarity and conviction.

For instance, if someone fears a job loss, creating a plan B could involve updating their resume, networking with industry contacts, or even exploring alternative career paths. This proactive stance empowers individuals, transforming a paralyzing fear into a motivating force. Moreover, preparation fosters resilience. When we prepare for the worst, we learn to adapt and respond effectively to various situations rather than being thrown off balance by unexpected events. This adaptability not only reduces anxiety but also enhances our confidence.

Here are some strategies you can try to help ease your fear of the unknown:

Focus on the Positive: Change is frequently met with apprehension because we naturally gravitate toward what we know. But what if we viewed change as something inherently beneficial? Rather than seeing it merely as a disturbance in our usual routine, we could recognize it as a vibrant tapestry filled with growth opportunities.

When faced with changing circumstances—whether in our personal lives or professional arenas—we are presented with a unique chance to evolve. This shift in perspective allows us to uncover potential benefits that may have previously escaped our notice. For instance, the discomfort that comes with change can drive us to acquire new skills, pushing us beyond our previous limits. Each new challenge we face acts as a catalyst for personal development, enhancing our adaptability and resilience. Embracing change as an opportunity means actively seeking out the silver linings. Perhaps a sudden shift in your career leads you to explore a role you had never considered before, unveiling hidden talents and interests.

Embrace Change as Normal: Change is inevitable and ongoing within most organizations, a vital component of growth and adaptation in our rapidly evolving world. It is crucial to recognize that embracing change can serve as a strength rather than a weakness. By anticipating and accepting the shifts that occur, whether due to advancements in technology, shifts in market demand, or internal restructuring, we position ourselves to respond more effectively.

Accepting change really sets the stage for our team members to become more resilient and adaptable, creating a vibrant culture where innovation can truly thrive. Rather than feeling caught off guard by sudden changes, our proactive approach helps us embrace the journey instead of pushing back against it. By nurturing this mindset, everyone—both individuals and teams—can dive into creative solutions and have open, constructive conversations about the adaptation processes we're experiencing.

Focus on What You Can Control: Amidst life's unpredictable tides, it is vital to direct our focus toward the actions and attitudes we can control. These elements create the foundation of our personal agency, empowering us to traverse the complexities of life with a renewed sense of purpose and clarity. By concentrating on what is within our power, we cultivate resilience, which acts as a bulwark against the continuous waves of external change that can often leave us feeling adrift and overwhelmed.

When we anchor ourselves in these controllable aspects, we not only ground ourselves but also empower our responses to the world around us. This steadfast dedication encourages a mindset that fosters growth and adaptability, transforming potential anxiety into a constructive force. In these moments, we can embrace the fluidity of life with a composed spirit, recognizing that while we may not dictate the currents of change, we certainly command our course through them. It is this balancing act—between accepting external circumstances and asserting our own influence—that ultimately enriches our journey, empowering us to meet challenges head-on with grace and confidence.

Experiment and Iterate: In the ever-evolving landscape of our professional lives, it's completely understandable to feel hesitant about embracing new strategies. However, it's important to see that stepping out of our comfort zones isn't just a risk; it's often a wonderful opportunity for growth and discovery. In the journey of life and professional growth, taking calculated risks is not merely advisable; it's essential. Imagine standing on the precipice of opportunity, where the unknown beckons with promises of innovation and personal development. To take a calculated risk means to weigh the potential outcomes thoughtfully and to step forward with intention rather than recklessness. It's about exploring new avenues, embracing creativity, and trying out new methods that could lead to remarkable breakthroughs.

Every great achievement begins with a decision to venture beyond the familiar. Whether it's in your career, personal projects, or the pursuit of hobbies, fear of failure can often grip us. However, it's crucial to remember that if you hesitate and allow uncertainty to dictate your actions, there will always be someone else willing to seize those opportunities. They will take the leap, explore the uncharted waters, and perhaps reach the success you aspired to achieve.

To thrive, we must cultivate a mindset that welcomes experimentation. This means trying new things, whether adopting new technologies, exploring unconventional approaches, or simply shifting our perspective on a familiar problem. While each new endeavor may not yield immediate success, it often provides invaluable lessons that contribute to our growth. There is a saying, "Fail fast, Learn fast."

Plan B

Even when we give our all and shine as top performers, it's tough to face the fact that a business might still make the tough decision to close for reasons beyond our control. That's why having a plan B is so important. It helps us feel more secure in a constantly changing workplace and ensures we're ready for whatever comes next. A backup plan is our safety net for unexpected events like layoffs, restructuring, or shifts in company direction, empowering us to steer our careers in a positive direction. Lately, many people have embraced part-time businesses or hobbies, and these can be transformed into full-time ventures when we need to shift to our plan B. It's all about being prepared and staying proactive. Let's explore some great ways to develop a Plan B.

- The most critical thing is to have a financial cushion. Aim to set aside three to six months of living expenses to cover essentials if you need to transition between jobs. Also, reserve funds specifically for training, certifications, or courses. Investing in yourself can strengthen and make your Plan B more feasible.
- Decide what you want your backup plan to achieve—whether it's a specific job role, industry, or lifestyle goal, like working remotely or achieving work-life balance. Sometimes, opportunities that don't follow a traditional career path can be the most rewarding. Stay flexible and consider roles in startups, remote work, or freelancing.
- Build relationships with people in other departments or industries. Networking expands your options for new opportunities, mentorship, or advice if you need to pivot. Stay active on LinkedIn or in industry-specific forums where potential collaborators,

mentors, or hiring managers can see your work and expertise.

- Imagine what you would do if there were a sudden job change. How would you want to respond? Visualizing a calm and proactive approach can help reduce fear if changes happen. Change can be challenging, but maintaining a positive attitude and resilient mindset can help you see setbacks as growth opportunities. Mental resilience will give you the confidence to transition smoothly if needed.

A well-thought-out Plan B empowers you to face uncertainty with confidence. By proactively developing a diverse skill set, building a strong network, and maintaining financial stability, you ensure that you're ready for whatever comes next. Embrace the idea of continuous growth and learning, and stay adaptable as you navigate an ever-evolving workplace. With a solid backup plan, you're not only prepared for change, you're ready to thrive in it.

<u>Exercise</u>

Task 1: List out all of your current skills, certifications, and experiences. Identify those transferable to other roles or industries and note any skills gaps that could limit your options.

Task 2: Analyze the last time you did something new for the first time.

Task 3: Discuss with peers in your organization and others about their Plan B.

Task 4: Create a Plan B and continuously reassess it.

Embracing Change: Your Path to Growth and Resilience

As you reach the end of this book, remember that growth and resilience are within your reach, no matter the environment or challenges ahead. New technologies, company reorganizations, and market shifts can be daunting, but with focus and persistence, you can not only survive but thrive. Embrace change as an opportunity, stay committed to continuous learning, and align with your organisation's evolving needs. Every challenge is a chance to prove your adaptability and strengthen your skills. With the right mindset, you are prepared to navigate and succeed in any career landscape.

You can contact me at [vinaysaini.author@gmail.com]. I'm happy to offer further help, engage in meaningful discussions, or hear your feedback and suggestions. Your thoughts are invaluable and inspire me to continue contributing to this journey of growth and learning.

Wishing you all the best on your journey of growth and success.

Warm regards,
Vinay Saini